Witchstones

By Wendy Trevennor

Green Magic

Green Magic
5 Stathe Cottages
Stathe
Somerset
TA7 0JL
England

www.greenmagicpublishing.com
info@greenmagicpublishing.com

Typeset by Green Man Books, Dorchester
greenmangallery@lineone.net

ISBN 978-0-9561886-9-4

GREEN MAGIC

This book is dedicated with humble gratitude to my mentor Kes, without which it would not be.

Foreword

Is this book for you? To use the Witchstones you do not have to be an initiated Wiccan, just someone who feels the call of the ancient wisdom, or a need to look beyond the present and mundane. This book has not been written just for those who have a great deal of knowledge of Wicca, although obviously it has been written by a Wiccan and does refer to Wiccan matters. I hope it is written in such a way as to make these references easily understood by anyone where they are pertinent to the subject.

In truth the main prerequisite for reading this book is curiosity about and attraction to this fascinating discipline. Runes generally are one of the most ancient, tangible and easily accessible tools of the Craft, and mastering their meaning and use is important to anyone wanting to go further in it. To master them, and then to go on and develop your own personal system is an exciting and satisfying project for anyone who wants to follow the Way of the Wise.

Contents

Introduction

Modern man looks into the future largely without fear. He looks ahead and sees that his life seems to be mapped out: school, college, work, marriage, children, pension and painless passing into spirit (assuming he believes in an afterlife) at a ripe, well-medicated old age. He does not expect to die at 25 from plague or (if female) childbirth, or to be swept up in a war fought with swords and bows, or starve to death because his crops have failed.

Perhaps this absence of fear is the reason most people in the modern age do not really live in the present, which passes almost unnoticed in the minutiae of everyday living. They live in the next moment, the next day or the next week; always looking forward. 'I'll go for a coffee in a short while.' 'What shall I have for dinner?' 'What time can I safely leave the office?' 'How shall I handle that meeting in the morning?' 'I can't wait until my holidays.' 'Next year I can have the conservatory done.' These sorts of thoughts sum up the way modern people in the western world experience their lives. Only in animals, children and the very old do we see individuals living from moment to moment, experiencing time at its living present moment.

Once man's fascination with the future and what it held for him did have its basis in fear. Our early ancestors did not worry about whether they would meet a dark, attractive stranger as much as they worried that the stranger would kill them or take their wife or livestock, or be the vanguard for some invasion by aggressive foreigners from the next valley. They also feared that they would in some way through their ignorance displease the Gods, who would punish them. In ages when disease, war, crop and game failure and sheer human lawlessness could destroy you tomorrow, those who promised a peek into the future were powerful and sought-after people, people to be propitiated. Their words were taken seriously and their advice followed.

But even now that vaccinations, peace treaties, agrochemicals and the police force have taken the sting out of much of the dark ancestral terrors that haunted our forebears, still our fascination with divination remains. Fortune-telling is as popular as ever, to judge by the profusion of advertisements in newspapers, magazines, the Internet, and the cards in shop windows for psychic, tarot, astrological and numerology readings. Even if for most people in the western world foreseeing the future means a glance at their horoscope over coffee, they still look, they ponder, they idly watch throughout the day for the promised sign, the piece of good fortune, the chance encounter, the warned-of minor catastrophe. Even such half-belief proves us to be the direct descendants of the ancient pagans who sought out the wise-man and asked his trance-given advice on their future.

From the earliest times, as archaeology shows, our forebears practised diverse methods of divination. Stones and bones were thrown and the patterns they fell in observed. The movements of animals, birds, the weather and tides were watched. Living things were killed and disembowelled, and the patterns of their viscera were read in the same way old Auntie Maude might read the tea-leaves. Wise men practised scrying in water, in oil, in fire and smoke, in clouds and in crystals. They used drugs to alter their consciousness, drugs discovered back in the mists of time and distilled from plants and fungi.

Astrology, always at the heart of foretelling, was developed around the middle of the second Millennium BCE by the Babylonians, later spreading to the Middle East and Greece, where early systems were already being formed. Later still Babylonian astrology merged with the Egyptian system to form the horoscopic astrology we know today.

Many ancient systems of divination exist and are still practised among the wise. Some rely on ancient alphabets, such as the Futhark and the Ogham, some on other symbols drawn from the human subconscious, including the Tarot and I-Ching. The very human body itself is read, the lines on the palm, the bumps on the head, the aura. Birthdates and the letters of names are dissected to give information. It has to be admitted that a lot of this is done commercially and for fun. Most people, asked about fortune-telling, have a vision of Gypsy Rose at the fairground, asking for her palm to be crossed with silver, or fortune cookies in Chinese restaurants, or Auntie Maude again with her inverted cup.

For those of us with metaphysical leanings divination means so much more. It is contact with the Eternal, one more method for spiritual development, even a form of prayer. For those of us who possess the tools; the rune-stones, the scrying mirror, the Tarot cards, the crystal dowsing pendulum, just touching them is like having a direct line to deity, the Pagan version of the Christian fondling his Book of Common Prayer in his pocket. What possibilities open before us when we take out our dowsing crystal from its bag, or carefully unwrap our scrying mirror from the black velvet cloth in which we keep it safely stowed. Part of this sense of awe comes from the sheer age of the traditions. Tarot goes back to the Mediaeval era – who knows if it is older? I Ching is over 4,000 years old, the runes go back to our Germanic ancestors of around 150CE; a sense of ancient times and ancient wisdom pervades these systems and their techniques.

It is surely only fitting that Wicca, whether you consider it ancient or modern, has its own traditional method of divination: the Witch's Runes. How old they are nobody seems to know. Vague murmurs of Ancient Egypt and Gypsy traditions surround them. But they are an ancient system going back, Goddess only knows how far, old enough to have spawned at least three versions, which is some measure of age!

Many years ago I was struggling to develop my own system, playing around with using astrological symbols, or animals or colours. Then I saw the Witch's Runes briefly described, with illustrations, in a book by Marian Green (*The Gentle Arts of Aquarian Magic*, Aquarian Press 1987), and was immediately intrigued by them. Her system uses 13 runes, which do not altogether match up with the 'regular' system; for example her set includes a rune called Time and another called the Whirling Wheel, which I have not seen in any other system. Marian speaks of using these runes with 'gentleness', opening your mind to them and to any new meanings they may introduce because they are a living and growing system. Later I also read *Lid Off The Cauldron*, a Wiccan handbook penned by a great lady of the Craft, Patricia

Crowther, who was taught about the runes by a Gypsy lady who called at her door. Rhiannon Ryall, in her fascinating book *West Country Wicca*, in which she writes of her enviable upbringing in a traditional pagan community, calls them 'tell-stones'. She describes nine stones: gate, water, even-armed cross, door, ring, gold spot, moon, silver spot and apple, which seem roughly to correspond with the system as we know it.

Looking at the different variations on the system, I was inspired to create my own set of witchstones, and as I used them, to add to them where I felt this was needed. Later still, when after 20 years of hedgewitchery, I was at last initiated by a Gardnerian/ Alexandrian High Priest, I saw the stones being used by my magical mentor, a hereditary High Priestess. I showed her the witchstones I had created myself, and was astonished when she picked up each one and told me its meaning. She admired them and advised me to write about them, and this book was born.

I have studied what little material is available on this tradition, and more importantly have studied the runes themselves. Writing this book has been a journey of discovery for me, as I hope it will be for you. Always I have loved the witch's tools; to make them, to decorate and personalise them, to handle them and use them is a delight for any witch. To do so makes them really yours, which in turn makes them more efficacious. The purpose of this book is to introduce you to this delight, to show you how to develop and personalise your own witchstones so that they become truly your own system, unique to you. I will start by attempting to give you a working knowledge of the Witch's Runes and to set you upon the path they open, to self-discovery and confidence in your own powers. Then together we will explore the path that opens up before us, a path I have already walked, but which I hope will bring blessings and inspiration to you.

When speaking of witches, for the sake of brevity I have used the female pronoun throughout. Of course witches can be male as well as female, and I hope any male witch reading this takes no offence, but understands that he is included in every reference to witches. Being one of the Wise, he will understand and forgive my wish to avoid the clumsiness of using 'he/she' at every turn.

1. The Traditional Witchstones

Because of the constant confusion with the traditional Craft chant called The Witches' Rune, as well as with the Futhark runes, I have chosen to refer to the stones by this name throughout the text.

Many Wiccans possess a set of these stones, a lesser known tool of the Craft, certainly less well known than the famous Futhark runes. Like the runes, they are personal to the owner, ancient in origin and can be used for divination, using several methods, magic or meditation. Unlike the runes, they are not alphabetical.

How far back the Witchstones go, no one seems to know. Some of the symbols seem to resonate with Ancient Egyptian hieroglyphs, notably the Eye, which looks a lot like the Egyptian symbol Wadjet, the Eye of Horus, (but then, so would any eye symbol). The Wave is often drawn as a spiral or set of spirals, which resemble the cup-and-ring markings found on ancient standing stones in the west, but a spiral is not a difficult pattern to draw and certainly not confined to Celtic carvings. Because the signs are very simple, they are harder to assign to any culture, ancient or newer. We cannot know for sure, so it is easier just to say that they are old, and concentrate on using them and their wisdom rather than worrying about how old.

Two main traditions exist for the Witchstones, a set of eight and a set of 13, (both are numbers associated with, and sacred to, Wicca).

In the set of eight, which seems to be of older provenance, each of the Witchstones corresponds to one of the eight Sabbats. This can give simple answers if the querent has asked about the timescale indicated in a reading. The stones are also allocated a simple answer, and are male or female. All may be relevant to a simple or complex reading.

The Witchstones seem to follow a fairly short time span. Unlike Tarot or astrology, which can speak of the far distant future, months or years away, the Witchstones seem to give answers that look no further than a few days into the future, which makes them ideal to use every day for simple 'what will my day bring today?' questions.

The set of 13 corresponds to the traditional maximum number for a coven, and includes many of the same symbols as the eight, plus some additional ones, but I have also seen sets where the simple eight is expanded to 12 by the addition of four stones representing the elements; fire, water, earth and air, or to 13 by the addition of a fifth extra rune representing spirit.

The stones have loose planetary correspondences and can be aligned with cards from the Major Arcana of the Tarot, with a little insight. The symbols are simple and easy to reproduce, and have traditional colours associated with them. They are symbols our forefathers would have recognised and resonated with: heavenly bodies, symbols of harvest, natural objects, symbols that go on with meaning forever, as long as there are people to understand them.

The Eight Runes

Often called the Gypsy Runes, the set of eight usually consists of the Sun, the Moon, the Rings, the Arrows (sometimes crossed), the Wave, the Birds, the Harvest (sometimes called the Ear of Corn or the Tree), and the Flight. These may be simply carved or drawn in black or in a colour that contrasts with the surface of the stones.

Here is a list of the eight Witchstones, with some of their correspondences.

Pagans living in the southern hemisphere will note that for them the dates of the Sabbats change. Their midsummer day is 21ˢᵗ December, midwinter is 21ˢᵗ June, and the other seasons change in like fashion. I have indicated their dates in italics and brackets.

The Sun.

A simply drawn depiction of the Sun with rays, usually coloured gold or yellow, this stone represents the power of the Sun and its influence on your life. It can also indicate a 24-hour period. Its gender is male and its number is one. Its simple answer, when drawn to ask a 'yes or no' question, is yes. This rune corresponds to the Sabbat Yule, the winter solstice on or around 21ˢᵗ December *(21ˢᵗ June)*. You may find it strange that the Sun would be associated with this, rather than the summer solstice, but there are good reasons in pagan belief. Midsummer marks the beginning of the *death* of the Sun; with the dawning of the longest day comes the start of his decline. On Midwinter day, the Sun rises for the first time to rebirth, as the days start to lengthen and he gains strength. It is his birthday, an idea which resonates with the Christian idea of a special child born at this time.

Meaning: this stone signifies strength, power, success and confidence, a man of authority, a father. It can also mean a male child, like the Star Child who is born on 21st December to grow up as the Sun God. It can mean the overcoming of past difficulties and achievement of goals, or healing. The astrological sign associated with this rune is Leo and the vibration is Apollo; leadership, art, music, healing.

The Moon.

A crescent moon drawn in white or silver, often with little stars scribed inside its outline, this stone represents the psychic and feminine influence of the moon in all her aspects. It can also indicate the period of a month. Its gender is female and its number is two. Its simple answer is no. This rune is associated with the Sabbat Imbolc, the only Sabbat dedicated to the Goddess alone, which falls on 1st or 2nd February *(1st or 2nd August)*. At this festival the Goddess is celebrated in all her aspects in the guise of Bride, a Celtic triple Goddess who is maiden, mother and crone. Christians know her as St Brigit.

Meaning: this stone is all things to do with the feminine; a woman in the question, femininity, the flow of the tides, feminine knowledge and wisdom, magic and madness, dreams, psychic and occult awareness. The astrological sign associated with this rune is Cancer, ruled by the Moon and associated with women's mysteries. The Threefold Goddess rules this rune, which has strong associations with your spiritual life.

The Rings
(sometimes called Empathy).

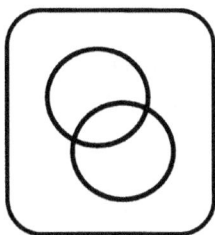

Two interlocking gold rings (some versions have three). Its gender is male and its number is three. Its simple answer is 'unknown'. This rune is associated with the Sabbat Beltane, the sacred marriage of the Goddess and God, which takes place at the end of April and beginning of May *(October/November)*. Most people today would recognise the celebrations associated with May Day; our ancestors celebrated this with dancing, feasting and sexual adventures, and even today Beltane is a traditional time for handfastings (pagan weddings).

Meaning: this rune is all about partnerships, whether romantic or not. It speaks of things coming together and joining, of harmony and sharing. In a relationship it can represent love or marriage. It can also mean business partnerships, agreements, contracts and alliances. It can also "tie together" two nearby symbols. This rune has a very loose astrological link to Mercury and Venus, the planets respectively of business, travel and communication, and love, fertility and wealth.

The Arrows
(sometimes called War or the Crossed Spears, sometimes the Crossroads).

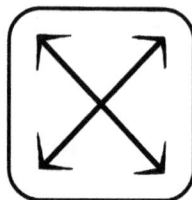

Two arrows, usually shown crossed, sometimes just in the air about to intersect. They are coloured bright red. The gender is male and the number four. Its simple answer is yes. This rune corresponds to the Sabbat Litha, the summer solstice around 21st June *(21st December)*, when pagans in the UK become more visible as they celebrate, gathering at ancient sites such as Stonehenge and Avebury to greet the sunrise on the longest day. Actually, contrary to popular belief, they are not celebrating the Sun's rise, but thanking him for his sacrifice and the good fortune they hope to enjoy through the summer, acknowledging his selfless decline towards death. For pagans the real celebration is at Yule, when the sun rises again after the longest night, born to renewed life and strength as the Star Child or Child of Promise.

Meaning: this rune points to troubles ahead, illness, mechanical breakdown, quarrels and other misfortunes. It also carries the meaning that these are not insurmountable, but traditionally this has been a rune of ill omen. In versions where the Crossroads replaces the Arrows, the rune still has an ominous feel about it. Something is about to happen, something that will change your plans, cause you difficulties and force choices on you.

The astrological sign associated with this rune is Aries, and the planet Mars. Its deepest meaning is challenge.

The Wave
(also sometimes called the Snake).

A curved line that may look like a breaking wave, a spiral or a collection of wiggly lines, and should be coloured marine blue. The gender is male and the number is five. The simple answer is no. The Wave corresponds to the Sabbat Ostara, the time of conception, on the Vernal Equinox on or around 21st March *(21st September)*. The Goddess conceives the Star Child – like many women in ancient times she is pregnant before her wedding, and the image of the great seas speaks of her womb and its promise.

Meaning: this rune speaks of travel, partings, longer journeys even, as its symbol conveys, across the sea. It shows a move away from your present environment, which may be just a change of habit rather than a physical move. It speaks of dreams and ambitions, and even returns, revenge or sacrifice. Being associated with water, it speaks of emotions and family, perhaps family secrets or inheritances, as well as any real associations with water and the sea.

The astrological sign associated with this rune is Pisces and the planet Neptune, bringer of dreams.

The Birds
(also called Freedom).

The symbol is three wiggly or V-shaped lines that look like three birds in flight, either exactly parallel or spaced out in a group as illustrated. The gender is female and the number is six. The simple answer is 'unknown'. The Birds correspond to the 'second harvest' at Mabon, the autumnal equinox around 21st September *(21st March)*. This Sabbat is a time of thanksgiving for the year and its gifts.

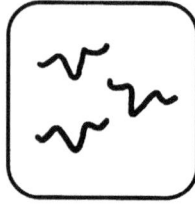

Meaning: the Birds speak of news, word from friends, letters, phone calls and small gifts. They speak of short journeys and ideas. They indicate that you can achieve your desires. The astrological sign associated with this rune is Gemini and the planet Mercury, god of travel and messages.

Harvest
(sometimes also the Tree or the Grain, or Nature).

This is shown as either an ear of wheat, a leaf, a complete tree or a vague symbol that could be any of these. The colours are green and gold. The gender is male and the number seven. The simple answer is yes.

Harvest corresponds to the Sabbat Lughnasadh, on 1st or 2nd August *(1st or 2nd February)*, better known to non-Wiccans as Lammas. This major Sabbat is concerned with harvest and the first corn and bread, and with the sacrifice of the God who is cut down with the grain on this date, to rise again later in the year.

Meaning: blossoming and expansion, prosperity and achievement, a harvest after work and planning. It indicates happiness and the natural flow of nature. The astrological sign associated with this rune is Sagittarius and the planet Jupiter, so it also speaks of success in lawsuits and conveyancing, help from authority.

Flight
(Confusingly, some sets call the Birds by this name. Sometimes called simply The Black Rune).

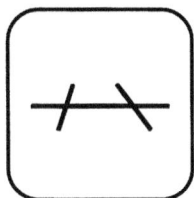

A straight line crossed by two shorter lines, drawn in black, or it may appear as The Scythe or the Sickle, with a simple line-drawing of a sickle or billhook, or just as a plain black surface. The gender is female and the number eight. The simple answer is no. Flight is related to the Sabbat Samhain, universally known as Halloween, a festival of the dead, and the Celtic New Year. At this time of year, so the ancient – and modern - pagans believed, the curtain between this world and the next was thinner, allowing contact with the unknown.

Meaning: this stone speaks of an ending, and the stones nearby will indicate whether it will be for good or ill. Like the Tarot card Death, it is an alarming symbol to draw, but it may not necessarily mean misfortune or death. It could be the ending of a relationship or a way of life that could actually bring good into your life. This Witchstone is associated with Saturn influences.

Pronunciation:

Many of the Wiccan Sabbats have names drawn from the Celtic languages, which have spellings that look quite difficult to our eyes. Here is a guide on how to pronounce them:

Yule - Yool
Imbolc – IMM-olk
Ostara – o-STAR-a
Beltane – BELL-tane
Litha – LITH-a, with the first syllable rhyming with 'myth'
Lughnasadh – loo-NASS-a
Mabon – MAY-bon
Samhain – SAV-een or SOW-een
Bride – Breed

Element Stones.

Element stones are designed to be used as an expansion of five further stones to add to a set of Witchstones. Each element also has its meanings and its set of correspondences.

Earth.

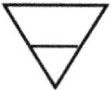

The element stones are usually inscribed with the symbol of the appropriate element; however these can vary. Earth may be, as depicted, a triangle with point downwards, or it may be a cross within a circle. A short line may be inscribed under the symbol to show which way up it should be, and if colours are used the symbol should be in brown or green. Simply painting the rune green or brown would also be quite correct.

The element of Earth is considered feminine.
The simple answer for this Witchstone is no.
Meaning: this represents home, security, comfort, fertility, work, money, practicality and everyday matters.

Air.

If colours are used, this symbol should be in yellow. The element of Air is considered masculine.

The simple answer is yes.

Meaning: this represents the intellect. It stands for intelligence, authority, courage and mental energy, strength of will and organisational skills.

Fire.

The correct colour for this symbol would be red.
The element of fire is considered masculine.
The simple answer is yes.
Meaning: creativity, inspiration, motivation, intuition and enthusiasm, also career, business projects and new ventures.

Water.

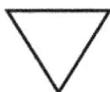

The colour would be blue, and the simple answer is no.
The element of Water is considered feminine.
Meaning: this represents the emotions, sensitivity, close personal

relationships, artistic ability, love, peace, contentment, fulfilment and happiness.

Spirit.

The colour would be purple/violet.
The simple answer is 'unknown'.
Meaning: this is your spiritual path, the spirit or soul, which is within all things. It speaks of the divine spark within us all and of the connectedness of things.

The Thirteen Runes

In addition to the Sun, the Moon, the Rings, the Arrows, the Wave, the Birds, The Harvest, and the Flight of the simple set of eight, the set of 13 has Man, Woman, Star, Romance and the Eye.

Man.

This and the Woman rune have as their symbols a rudimentary image of the respective genital areas. This rune speaks of the engorged penis, an upraised weapon such as a spear or sword, or is perhaps a crude line-drawing of the penis and testes. The Witchstone speaks of a man in the question, perhaps a stranger coming into your life, or a man you asked about when you cast the runes, a figure of authority, perhaps, or even a male baby.

Woman.

The symbol is the triangle of a woman's pudenda and thighs, the doorway of life as well as love. It represents a woman in the question, or is to do with women's matters, perhaps pregnancy, a new partner (if you are male or a gay woman), or a female child. It could be your mother, sister, wife or daughter, or a female stranger coming into your life. It speaks of feminine qualities such as softness, compassion, motherliness, caring.

Star.

The energies of this rune are to do with achievement, spiritual development, glory, fame; personal success on many levels, also high ideals, perhaps for a cause greater than yourself, wishes and dreams. Think about the word 'star' and its associations in our culture. A star is someone who has achieved fame and fortune through their own talent in the fields of acting, playing, singing or sport, someone who is special in some way, who stands out from the crowd. The rune speaks of achieving that success, of reaching the goal.

Romance.

This strange little glyph, somewhat resembling the multi-faith spiritual symbol triquetra and with a passing resemblance to a woman's internal or a man's external reproductive organs, speaks of love, romantic or erotic. It could be a new relationship entering your life, or a new spark or new development in an existing one. Unlike the Rings, it does not refer to partnerships of any other kind, such as business; it is solely concerned with the close emotional and physical relationship between two people, with passion and infatuation.

The Eye.

If you are creating your own set, you would paint the eye the same colour as your own, because it represents you, or the querent in the question. The Eye can be laid down before a cast, to act as a centre point for the cast, when runes will be read in relation to their nearness to the Eye. Or it can be cast as one of the set, when it speaks of a life-changing revelation, a message from Spirit, a 'Road to Damascus' scenario which will open your eyes to something very important to your future and your way of life. The Eye of God? Maybe. It will need to be read with nearby runes for a meaningful answer.

2. Understanding the System

The system outlined in the previous chapter might raise many questions in your mind. The meanings offered for the runes are so vague, you might think; sometimes you might not understand what is meant by certain phrases, and the meanings of the individual runes as written often seem to overlap. Don't worry: this book is all about showing you how to use, understand and make the most of your Witchstones. Reading the description of them is only the very first step.

I remember when I bought my first pack of Tarot cards when I was 20; they came in a nice little velvet pouch with a small booklet explaining what the different cards meant and how to lay them in a variety of different spreads. I bored all my friends rigid for weeks doing readings for them with the booklet in my hand, because I hadn't grasped that *knowing the stated meanings* of the cards didn't make me a Tarot reader.

Any experienced witch knows that you can't rely on a written list of meanings for any divinatory system; divination doesn't work like that. The runes themselves trigger associations in your subconscious, associations you might not even be aware of because they have their roots in our ancestral group consciousness. Or they may refer to something in your childhood you are no longer aware of, perhaps a detail from your bedroom wallpaper when you were very small, or an illustration from one of your favourite childhood books. Witches also know and use a body of knowledge called *Correspondences*, magically linked objects, colours, times, herbs, oils and crystals which can be used to evoke the correct vibration for a certain kind of spellwork. This is hard to explain to a non-Wiccan, but the feeling is that some items and essences go with certain energies, in the way that mint sauce goes with lamb, and doesn't go with chicken.

Let us take as an example the love goddess Venus. Using the energies of Venus would be good in a love spell, and she has her own set of correspondences. To raise Venus energies you might light pink candles, have roses on the altar and use a rose-scented incense. We instinctively *know* these associations, if we stop to think about them. Why are Valentine cards predominantly pink, why do they have roses on them, why do we send roses to a lover? (Yes, I know these days Valentine cards are more likely to be red; I think this has to do with the changing attitude towards sexuality in modern society. Red is the colour of Mars, who is concerned with lust rather than tender romantic feelings and old-fashioned courtship). Venus also rules fertility and wealth, and another of her colours is green. See what I mean?

For this reason I give a short list of correspondences below, which it would be a good idea to become familiar with if you want your rune reading to be really effective. Don't learn it by heart; just be happy that you know your way around it. Don't feel you have to be too much of a stickler about every little thing; magic and divination don't work like that.

For a percentage of people using the runes, the reading will arise from psychic intuition, in the same way a palm reader will often say that the actual lines on the hand are not what he or she really looks at; that he or she receives psychic impressions from holding the hand and opening the mind.

Correspondences

Here is a list of the planetary and element correspondences used in a witch's circle. Correspondences summon the right elements to your aid. We give these planetary names because this is traditional and because the images of the classical gods associated with them are easy to remember. Think of our old friend Venus again. There she stands, probably in the nude, perhaps with her arm held modestly over her perfectly-shaped bosom, her long golden hair streaming and her eyes beaming an invitation at any male who looks at her. You may well have got an instant flash of that most famous painting depicting her: Botticelli's Birth of Venus. She is beauty personified.

Using the correct correspondences for Venus will bring her influences into whatever you are doing. If it is a love spell, you are off to a flying start. If you are reading your witchstones, it will help if you know and recognise the signs connected with her.

To add another layer of understanding, the planets (in astrology this term includes the Sun and Moon) are all associated with the 12 signs of the Zodiac, which also have their own virtues and qualities. These are probably better known by the general public, who are often familiar with their own star signs and those of their friends and family.

Sun

Think of golden-haired Apollo, sitting up there on Mount Olympus strumming his lyre with one hand, writing poetry with the other and being impossibly handsome. Like the great Apollo, the Sun rules joy, pride, success, prosperity, promotion, leadership and advancement, as well as the arts, especially music and poetry, and healing. It is the planet of kings.

The virtues of Leo, the astrological sign ruled by the sun, are generosity, courage, daring, broad-mindedness and artistic ability, but I'm sorry to say that Leos can also be bossy and interfering control-freaks.

Think of all these attributes if you draw the Sun rune.

Day of the week: Sunday.
Colours: yellow, gold and sky-blue.
Metal: gold.
Gems: amber, carnelian, topaz or yellow diamond, tiger's eye, sunstone.
Also children, eagles, lions, hawks, the phoenix, cockerels, condors, parrots, sparrows, honey and bees, sunflowers and other sun-loving plants.
Tarot: the Sun.
Element: fire.
Number: one.

Moon

The Moon brings to the pagan mind the great Triple Goddess, the Maiden, Mother and Crone who rule women in all their stages of life. You can think of her as the Maiden, as the slender, fierce huntress Diana with her bow and hounds, or as Selene the Mother, gentle, fertile and wise, or as Hecate the Crone, a dark-robed, awe-inspiring figure of mystery encountered only in dreams and dark of night. The Moon rules cycles, tides, birth, poetry, generation and fertility, inspiration, travel especially by water, rain, the seas, intuition, magic, psychic ability, secrets, women's mysteries, dreams, inns and hotels, real estate, the food industry and impersonations.

The attributes of her astrological sign Cancer are swift changes of mood, an emotional and loving heart, the need to protect the home and family, and an imaginative and intuitive mind. Cancer is a water sign that brings to mind the Moon's association with the sea, with tides and mysteries and dreams. There is a strong association between this rune and the Wave rune.

Day of the week: Monday.

Colours: because the Moon has three different aspects, she is associated with (new) silver, white or pale grey, (full) red, (waning) black.

Metal: silver

Gems: moonstone, pearl and mother-of-pearl, rock crystal, quartz, abalone, aquamarine, opal, selenite.

Also hares and rabbits, cats, elephants, moths, shellfish, bats, snails, frogs, geese and swans.

Tarot: the Moon and the High Priestess

Element: water.

Number: three.

Mercury

The wing-footed messenger of the Gods crops up time and again in commercial logos and heraldry everywhere. We all immediately recognise his wide-brimmed winged hat and the funny wand he carries (the caduceus, composed of two snakes entwined around a staff) and associate them with speed, travel, deliveries and medicine. He rules travel and communication, intellect, business and commerce, writing, contracts, buying and selling, information of all kinds including Information Technology, wisdom, cleverness, creativity, science, particularly medical science, and memory.

Mercury rules two astrological signs, Virgo and Gemini. The sign of Virgo is well known for fussiness, perfectionism and worry, while Geminis are said to be two people in one, or at least to have that *mercurial* quality of changing from one mood to another in a trice.

Day of the week: Wednesday.

Colour: orange.

Metal: mercury or aluminium.

Gems: opal, moss agate, onyx, carnelian, citrine, fluorite.

Also: hermaphrodites (that's people or animals that combine both genders), jackals, twin serpents, foxes and vixens, snakes, monkeys, hyenas.

Zodiac: Virgo and Gemini.

Tarot: The Hanged Man.

Element: air.

Numbers: one, two, four and eight.

Venus

The love-goddess (we've already met her!) rules love and relationships, pleasure, female sexuality, the Arts, music, beauty (in fact many things involving an element of vanity or a bit of showing off), luxury, scent, social affairs, harmony, friendship, attraction, material possessions and money, wealth, fertility, the fashion and beauty industry, actors, performers, TV, radio and film performers.

The attributes of her astrological sign of Taurus include physical beauty, a warm, loving heart, and a placid, patient character, while her other sign, Libra, represents balance and harmony.

Day of the week: Friday.
Colour: green and pink.
Metal: copper.
Gems: emerald, rose quartz (Venus rules the acquisition of all gems), amber, malachite, jade.
Also: doves, lynxes, bees, butterflies, peacocks, household pets, singing birds, sheep, scented flowers, especially roses.
Tarot: The Empress and The Lovers.
Element: earth and water.
Number: six.

Mars

This ancient war god rules passion, force, power, lust, courage, strength of will, the military, physical exertion, machinery, and competition, male sexuality, anger, destruction, medical issues, surgery, conflict, sports. The Greeks and Romans saw him as a great muscular man clad in armour and blood-red tunic, and brandishing his weapons, a stranger to fear and timidity and the very opposite of his romantic partner Venus.

The attributes of his astrological sign Aries are ferocious energy, determination, courage and assertiveness, so this is a warrior.

Day of the week: Tuesday.
Colour: red.
Metal: iron and steel.
Gems: ruby, garnet, bloodstone, jasper.
Also: rams and bulls, bulldogs.
Tarot: The Tower, Strength.
Element: fire.
Number: five.

Jupiter

The benign and pleasure-loving ruler of the Olympian Gods has given his Roman name to the term jovial (with the oddities of Latin grammar his name can also sometimes be written as Jove), which sums up his character. If you imagine a sort of pagan Father Christmas, presiding over a huge feast and enjoying every moment, you will have a good idea of the personality of this deity. Yet he could also be angry, if aroused, and was wont to hurl thunderbolts at people who had trodden on his toes! He rules good living, success, abundance, money, investments, ambition, growth, parties and social gatherings, leadership and politics, power, royalty, legal judgements, luck, the seeking and granting of favours. He is the ultimate symbol of royalty, dignity and authority.

Jupiter rules the astrological sign Sagittarius; people with this birth-sign are said to be jovial, honest, bluff and outspoken, and to love good food and good living.

Day of the week: Thursday.

Colour: blue (deep or royal), purple.

Metal: tin, bronze.

Gems: lapis lazuli, amethyst, turquoise, sapphire.

Also: oak trees, the unicorn, deer and other game.

Tarot: The Wheel of Fortune, Justice and the Emperor.

Element: fire and earth.

Number: four and five.

Saturn

I always think of Saturn as a bit like Eeyore in Winnie-the-Pooh, a bit of a drag, rather earthbound, grim and pessimistic. This influence is very subterranean and rules land and real estate, past lives, lies, losses, learning life's lessons, banks, debts, institutions, obstacles, limitations, binding, time and death. He can be associated with the recovery of debts, with building and farming, also with pain and loss. And yet he is also deeply associated with our modern festival of Christmas, known by the Romans as Saturnalia, a public holiday and time of great jollity.

His astrological sign is Capricorn, which is known for pessimism, patience and prudence.

Day of the week: Saturday.
Colours: black, brown, dark grey, blue.
Metal: lead, pewter.
Gems: onyx, black tourmaline, obsidian, hematite, jet.
Also: many sinister and poisonous plants such as hemlock, henbane, ivy, nightshade and wolfsbane, crows, ravens, goats and cloven-footed animals such as pigs.
Tarot: The World and Death.
Element: earth.
Numbers: three and seven.

Uranus

Uranus is the planet of the magician, one whose mind is unique and can cause magical changes. It rules unexpected changes, revolutions, sovereignty, originality, higher consciousness, metaphysics, new inventions, clairvoyance, freedom, eccentricity and independence. If you want a mental picture, think of the magician from the sketch in Disney's Fantasia, with his eyes blazing and sparks and fire trailing from his wand.

Remember everyone getting all excited about the Age of Aquarius, back in the 1960s? Aquarius is the sign ruled by Uranus, and it is the sign of magic and inspiration.

Colours: blue, electric blue, violet, yellow.
Metal: uranium.

Gems: zircon, amber, amethyst, garnet, aventurine, diamond.
Also: alligator, crocodile, boar, bear, cat.
Tarot: The Magician.
Element: air.
Numbers: seven and ten.

Neptune

Here he is, basking on the surface of the sea in his seashell-shaped chariot drawn by dolphins, trident in one hand, his long blue beard encrusted with sea-gems and sea-shells, the mysterious ruler of the oceans. His eyes sparkle like sunlight on waves, and if you look deeper into them, with the knowledge of the boundless oceans and their mysteries.

He rules inner vision and perception, intuition, inspiration, dreams, divination, strangely enough horse-racing, sea-travel and sea-industries including fishing, mining and oil-drilling.

Neptune rules the astrological sign of Pisces. Pisceans are imaginative, sensitive daydreamers.

Colours: blue, blue-green, purple, white.
Metal: iron, bronze.
Gems: sapphire, amethyst, coral, jade, pearl and mother-of-pearl.
Also: all sea animals and sea plants, fish, crustaceans, octopi, sea-birds.
Tarot: The Emperor.
Element: water.
Numbers: eight and twelve.

Pluto

This ruler of Hades is associated with the unconscious and buried emotions, and rules death and rebirth, secrets and wealth, transformations, astral travel, the otherworld, self-knowledge, spirituality, sexuality, transfigurations and metamorphosis. Think of buried treasure – this will be the sort of thing Pluto would rule, whether it is a rotted chest full of gold doubloons or a wonderful secret revealed. If you want a picture of him, think of the Walt Disney animated film Hercules, in which the muscle-bound hero contends with the sinister sarcastic villain Hades (his Greek name).

Pluto rules the Zodiac sign Scorpio, said to give determined, forceful personality traits with personal magnetism and a tendency to be secretive.

Colours: dark red, brown, black, grey, purple.
Metal: tin or steel.
Gems: topaz, ruby, jet, garnet, bloodstone, aventurine.
Also: fox.
Zodiac: Scorpio.
Tarot: The Pope/Hierophant.
Element: earth and water.
Numbers: nine, eleven, twelve and seventeen.

The Four Elements

In Wicca the four elements (five, with Spirit) are regarded as kingdoms of magical beings that live beside and among us, but not on the same plane. Treated with respect they can be powerful friends, but they can also punish those who offend them. They also represent the elements that make up our own beings: north is the physical body, east is the mind, south our courage and passion, and west our emotions.

Earth
The element of earth is considered to reside in the north, and rules the home, the body, nature and growth, fertility, fields and

agriculture, caves and caverns, rocks, standing stones, mountains, hills, wealth, jobs and material gain, birth, health, death, silence, stability.

The element is feminine.

Earth is associated with the north, with midnight and midwinter.

Zodiac: Capricorn, Taurus and Virgo.

Colours: green (or brown, black or white).

Humour: melancholy – cold and dry.

Animals and plants: the wolf, snake, cattle, owl, stag and wild cats.

Stones: onyx, jade, amethyst, and fluorite.

Air

This element rules the intellect, memory, all mental, intuitive and psychic work, knowledge, abstract learning, test-taking, theory, divination and psychic ability, windswept hills, plains, windy beaches, high mountain peaks, high towers, wind and breath, travel and overcoming addictions.

The element is masculine.

Air is associated with the east, with dawn and spring.

Zodiac: Gemini, Libra and Aquarius.

Colours: yellow (or pale blue and pastels generally).

Humour: sanguine – warm and moist.

Animals and plants: all birds and insects, bats, doves, the wolf, fox, deer, turtle and hare.

Stones: moonstone, turquoise and rhodochrosite.

Fire

This element rules energy, lifeblood, enthusiasm, inspiration, willpower, healing, combat, anger, desire, determination, success,

sex, illness, protection, legal matters, competitions and strength.
The element is masculine.

Fire is associated with the south, and with midday and midsummer.
Zodiac: Leo, Aries, Sagittarius.
Colours: red (or orange and gold).
Humour: choleric – hot and dry.
Animals and plants: salamanders, porcupines, coyotes, foxes, squirrels, hawk, mice, deer, bear, snakes, dragons, horses and lions. Scarlet flowers, berries and leaves, such as pyracantha, flowering almond, garlic, mustard, nettle, chillies, onions, red peppers.
Stones: fire opal, amber, citrine, smoky crystals, gold and copper.

Water

Water rules emotions and feelings, love, friendship, courage, daring, sorrow and partings, the unconscious mind, intuition, inspiration and art, travel, meditation, healing, dreams, childbirth, clairvoyance and purification.
The element is feminine.

Water is associated with the west, with sunset and autumn.
Zodiac: Cancer, Scorpio, Pisces.
Colours: blue (or blue-green, grey, indigo).
Humour: phlegmatic – cold and wet.
Animals and plants: all seaweeds and aquatic plants, willows and riverside plants. Fish and marine animals, whales, dolphins, seals, sea lions, etc., all sea birds and the raven. Night creatures. Frogs, newts and water insects.
Stones: sapphires, pearls and mother-of-pearl, aquamarines, river rocks, amethyst, coral, seashells, and rainbow coloured crystals. Silver.

Okay, what was all that about? Well, a witch would apply these correspondences, planets and elements, to the Witchstones to add another layer of meaning to them. It's a bit like putting little coloured stickers on items when you are having a tidy-up and want to know where various things belong. Now we can start applying these correspondences to the Witchstones, and hopefully this will start to bring you some understanding of their energies.

I have taken the full set of 13 Witchstones for this, and left out the element runes because they are already supplied with their own detailed set of correspondences. Here is a simple table for quick reference, followed by some more detailed descriptions in the next chapter. Don't worry that some of the windows are blank – these correspondences are quite loose, and you may not even agree with them once you start to develop your own system of Witchstones.

Witchstone	Planet	Zodiac sign	element	gender	energies
Sun	Sun	Leo	fire	male	positive
Moon	Moon	Cancer	water	female	neutral
Rings	Venus	Taurus and Libra		female	positive
Arrows	Mars	Aries	fire	male	negative
Wave	Neptune	Pisces	water	female	neutral
Birds	Mercury	Libra and Gemini	air	female	positive
Harvest	Jupiter	Sagittarius	fire	male	positive
Flight	Saturn	Capricorn	earth	female	neutral
Man	Sun/Mars		fire/air	male	neutral
Woman	Venus/Moon		earth/water	female	neutral
Star	Uranus	Aquarius		male	positive
Romance	Pluto	Scorpio		both	neutral
Eye					neutral

Planet sign element gender energies

28

3. A Discussion of the Symbols

Now let us finally go and meet each Witchstone properly, introduce ourselves and get to know these symbols which are going to be a part of our magical life. Building a working relationship with these traditional Witchstones will also help you when it comes to personalising your stones.

A very good way to create a good relationship with your Witchstones is to concentrate on one stone at a time, carry it around with you in your pocket or handbag for some days, meditate on it, sleep with it under your pillow. Take it out and look at it whenever you have a few moments to spare, allow your mind to tick over and see what comes to you from holding and looking at the stone. Read the sections below on each Witchstone, take them in and digest them as a starting point for your meditations. Notice what happens to you in the course of the day, who you meet, what you hear, what symbols you see along the way. Carry a little notebook with you, and make notes whenever something comes to you about the nature and meaning of this Witchstone. Do this with each of the Witchstones, one by one, until you feel you know them well.

Even after you have been using the stones for years, you may well find this continues to be a useful exercise. The Witchstones go on developing as you do, and will always have new and different things to teach you.

Sun

The Sun rune carries the energies of the element fire, and also those of the astrological planet sun, of course. But because we are now talking about the Witchstone Sun, we can't just trot out all the solar correspondences and leave it at that. Focus on the symbol itself, while keeping the sun correspondences in mind. What does it bring to mind? Sun energies have a definite personality, someone golden, charming, attractive, generous, brave, artistic and with leadership abilities. Someone who can be bossy and a little vain. Someone who is young, or has young energies. If it is a real person, it could even be someone with fair hair and blue eyes. Is this a person you know, or are asking a question about? Is it a situation, such as a possible promotion at work, or a hope or dream such as a holiday in the sun?

Although the rune speaks of a person with male energies, there are times when it could represent someone female, perhaps a female boss or someone who has sun energies in some other way, such as an artist or musician, or a striking lioness of a lady with a mane of tawny hair. It is not likely to ever represent someone who could be a threat to you, as it is a positive rune. Its positive energies can even charge adjacent runes with good meaning when you cast the Witchstones for a reading (later, later!). It speaks of good things, of success, healing, wealth and confidence. It speaks of light, truth and honesty, of open-mindedness and open-handedness.

Perhaps your mind may fall across a phrase which means something to you, such as 'a place in the sun', 'blue-sky thinking', a 'sunny personality', 'a sunny smile'. If the Witchstone has a message for you, you will recognise it if you open your mind to it.

Moon

The Moon also uses the correspondences for the planet moon, and carries the energies of water, which means it has a lot to do with emotions, dreams, psychic awareness and intuition. 'I feel it in my water', a person might say. This Witchstone is the Goddess's own symbol, and it speaks of magic, mystery, dreams and visions, inspiration, beauty and the occult. It could be indicating your spiritual path, and it strongly indicates your past, your family background and issues arising from your childhood. Madness may be in the equation too – it is something associated with the Moon and her powers. This could be the madness of obsessive love. The Moon is not necessarily a positive Witchstone, and she may indicate betrayal, secrets and lies.

If this rune indicates a female person, it will be a very different person from the lioness in the Sun description. The Moon speaks of age and wisdom, even if found in a young person. 'She has hidden depths', someone might say of this person, 'an old soul' or 'an old head on young shoulders'.

People whose horoscopes are ruled by the Moon, for example people with the Sun sign Cancer, often have a certain look about them. In an older person or a younger person with very fair colouring, a perfect, gleaming head of silvery pale or white hair is often associated with Cancer – I have often noticed this when casting horoscopes for people. But we are not saying the Moon rune conveys the meaning of an older person only because, as we know, the Moon represents three ages of women. This rune is just as likely to mean a fierce young girl, the huntress personified, or a mature motherly woman, or someone who, while not fitting these descriptions in terms of her age, has some of these qualities.

Open your mind, as with the Sun rune, to the possibilities, allow phrases to fall into your mind, as they will if you give them an opening. Think of phrases that have meaning for you: 'once in a blue moon', 'over the moon', 'promise the moon', 'moonlight and roses', or even 'moonstruck', 'moonshine' and 'moon madness'.

Rings

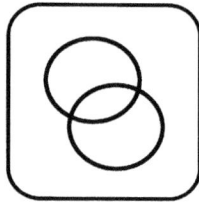

This Witchstone speaks for itself – golden rings are a symbol of love, romantic promises, betrothals, weddings and partnerships since time immemorial throughout the world. Advertisers have used it as a symbol of the promise of love – remember the Colgate® 'ring of confidence', implying that a girl who used this brand of toothpaste would meet and attract her future husband? The Rings have mildly positive energies; they speak of good times unless influenced by more threatening Witchstones nearby. Their meaning has to do with partnerships, rather than basic sex and attraction (which is indicated by the Romance Witchstone) and this can also mean business partnerships, agreements or legal contracts, and the stone can also tie together concepts that crop up in a reading to give a further layer of meaning. They speak of harmony and sharing, of allies and partners. The symbol of rings entwined speaks of long, happy marriages – 'they lived happily ever after' – of mutual plans and dreams, of wooing, white lace, honeymoons, anniversaries and the golden path walked hand-in-hand by loving elderly couples who have spent their lives together. Rings can also sometimes be magic – if you ever read fairy stories as a child (or an adult) you will know this. The Rings can also mean a promise, a very special one, such as the vows of a nun (nuns wear a wedding ring, as a symbol of their commitment to Christ) or to an organisation of some other kind, perhaps something like the Freemasons, who also wear rings to show their loyalty and commitment to their group.

Can they ever be negative? There could be circumstances in which marriage itself might be an encumbrance, if people have fallen out of love or have a partner who is faithless or domineering. Then perhaps the rings could take on a meaning more like a fetter, depending on the circumstances of the querent, and when negatively aspected. Married people sometimes jokingly say the wedding ring is a 'slave's bangle' or refer to it as a 'ring through their nose' if they are at odds with their partner.

Arrows/Crossroads

This Witchstone is the only one that carries totally negative energies, and yet there is still hope, even when it appears. The symbol of arrows speaks to us of annoyances, troubles, quarrels and injuries, of any sort of calamity or nuisance. As the Crossroads it shows that a choice will be forced on you, one not to your liking. Think of that moment in the movies, when the hero is trying to get in to see the King and plead for someone's life or remonstrate with him about his behaviour. The guards on either side of the door immediately clash their spears into a cross in front of him to block his way – there is a perfect image of the Crossed Arrows. Once a lethal weapon, the arrow has had its significance as a deadly weapon watered down by millennia of the gun and other more advanced weapons, and by its use as a symbol of way-finding. Arrows have also been associated benignly with Cupid, and the eyes of lovers. Yet it does stand as a symbol of misfortune, and when called the Crossroads, it stills speaks of ill omens, of foreboding, of shadows that lurk in the future. In Vodou the Loa Baron Kalfu, often called Carrefour (crossroads), one of the aspects of Papa Legba, is seen as a demon or associated with Satan. He allows or even helps the manifestation of bad luck, deliberate destruction, misfortune and injustice. In European tradition, suicides were buried at crossroads, often with a stake through their hearts, as a way to stop them haunting honest folk and because they were no longer considered deserving of Christian burial within the churchyard. Vampires and witches were seen as hanging around crossroads at night (personally, I have better things to do!), and woe to the foolish soul who found himself there at midnight.

Yet this Witchstone may not speak of unmitigated disaster and calamity, but of setbacks and irritations that can be overcome with patience and fortitude. The King's guards will move their spears aside when the royal hand is waved at them, and let the hero into the royal chamber to speak his mind. This stone has to do with occurrences that are sudden and seem threatening: arguments, quarrels, illnesses, accidents and injuries, confusion, mechanical breakdowns. It can mean rivalry, fights and violence. But it also carries the meaning that these are temporary problems, and that patience and perseverance will triumph in the end.

Wave

The mighty sea rolls on forever, hiding Goddess knows how many secrets, taking lives without pity or discrimination, moving in tides according to its own will and its ancient custom. It may bestow wealth beyond the dreams of man – or steal away your beloved, never to be seen again. Its bounty is as great as its mysteries, yet is not given without cost. The Vikings called it 'the Old Grey Widow-maker' and generations of sailors' wives have regarded it with fear and hatred. Yet it is also the sea of our childhood holidays, sparkling and blue with lacy white foam, giver of wet golden sand for castles, and rock pools for shrimp and tiny crabs, a beautiful paddling pool with built-in Jacuzzi. Some of our favourite literature is set on the sea; pirates maraud, heroes wage war and mad captains follow white whales across the briny billows. The English language is full of often unrecognised nautical expressions; we English regard ourselves as the monarchs of the sea, the sons of the sea. Going to sea, or running away to sea, is seen as a great adventure, an event to make a man of a boy, to broaden the mind and make his fortune.

The sea is magical: in Celtic literature 'water from the ninth wave' is a common ingredient for enchantment. Mysterious beings, mermaids and monsters, emerge at intervals to fascinate or terrify. Strange objects or bodies wash up on the shores. Things taken by the sea undergo a 'sea-change' and emerge as precious. Both fear and fascination are associated with the sea, treasures and losses, fish harvests and drownings.

This Witchstone speaks of travel, particularly long journeys and voyages across the sea, also of voyages of personal discovery, travel along your spiritual path or towards your personal destiny. In a way it is related to the Birds, for it speaks of news and travel, but these are much more momentous; news from afar and global travel, rather than back-door gossip and titbits. It speaks of partings, sacrifices and emotional reactions, of natural forces overwhelming people. And as the ocean often returns things long lost, it also speaks of karma, and of revenge, returns and inheritances. It is a powerful symbol.

Birds

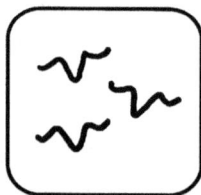

Birds have always been regarded as carrying messages (long before carrier pigeons). Ancient man watched the skies and noted the movements of birds as a method of divination, a significance they have kept in the subconscious to the present day. Birds speak of messages, gossip (a little bird told me), letters, phone calls, emails and news of friends. I know people who declare that a small present from a bird landing on one's head (splat!) is a promise of good luck. This Witchstone has a neutral to benevolent energy – I always feel myself that it is a nice stone to draw and carries good news with it, although the ancients would not have regarded birds as being always a good sign. Black birds, especially carrion birds like crows and ravens, because of their association with death and battlefields, got a bad press. The Irish regarded crows as fairy birds intent on mischief; some communities still regard it as an ill omen if a crow lands on your roof or other building. A 'murder of crows' is the name given to a group of these birds, and 'an unkindness of ravens' is another group name. 'Bird of ill omen' and 'storm-crow' are terms suggesting birds can be bringers of bad luck or bad news, and I have a friend – a faith healer and psychic, who made up with her ex-husband *after* his death – who regards even the robin in this way. She declares that when she sees the pretty little redbreast in her garden she knows someone in her family or acquaintance is going to die. Owls, too, have often been associated with ill-omen, particularly if they are about during the day. Take it away, Will:

'And yesterday the bird of night did sit
Even at noon-day upon the market-place,
Hooting and shrieking. When these prodigies
Do so conjointly meet, let not men say
'These are their reasons; they are natural;'
For, I believe, they are portentous things
Unto the climate that they point upon.'

(Julius Caesar, Act I, scene III)

Personally I don't think the Birds can carry negative energy unless they are aspected by strongly negative stones nearby. They speak of cheerful or mundane news, village gossip, a small outing or errand, a call from someone you haven't seen in a while, an idea, a postcard or even a small gift. Perhaps even a visit from the stork. I drew the Birds recently, while worrying about a friend who was waiting for test results on a lump in her neck. I had been very concerned for her, and when I drew this stone, my mind flew to her at once. I asked the Witchstones to clarify and drew another stone: the Sun. I knew then that she was going to be all right, and sure enough later that day I read her Facebook posts saying her tests had proved negative.

My own way of thinking of this symbol is as a bird bath in a sunny garden, where sparrows, starlings, tits, finches and wrens gather to drink, flutter their wings in the water and exchange chatter and gossip, or even as a carrier pigeon which appears from the distance bearing news.

Harvest

A fat, golden ear of corn is a symbol of achievement and riches in any language, speaking of waving fields of grain waiting to be made into bread to feed the community and fill the farmer's pockets. Even in its raw unprocessed state it almost makes one's mouth water, bringing to mind the scent of freshly baked bread or, perhaps more likely in the 21st century, the glossy fronts of cereal packets filled with over-processed and sugared breakfast carbs. Despite the bad press wheat has had recently with the rising levels of coeliac disease and IBS, not to mention glycaemic indexes, we all instinctively feel that grains are a healthy source of wholesome and excellent nutrition. Say the words 'wheat germ' and 'wholegrain' to yourself and see if it isn't so. Bread is a staple of our lives; the word has even been used in popular culture to signify money, a living wage.

This beneficent rune paints a picture of hard work, of men with sweat-stained shirts and sunburned arms and brows labouring in dusty fields – but with smiles on their faces and anticipation of the harvest home supper to come. It speaks of just desserts, of harvest after work, a goal achieved after planning, striving, even suffering. It says, 'You have worked hard for this, and you deserve it'.

In UK culture the month of August also says 'holidays', in the sense of a break after labouring all year in office, factory or school, something to look forward to and dream of during chilly days or periods of boredom or overwork.

Always positive, the Harvest rune speaks of prosperity and expansion, the flowering of plans, fruition, the pay-off. Your dream is about to come true, but you have earned it. This is not a gift from the Gods, but something you have achieved yourself through long planning, hard work, scrimping, saving and going without. You have become the breadwinner, the harvester, the gatherer of Golden Grain.

Flight

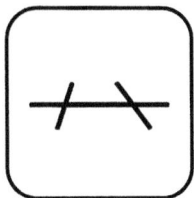

People who know very little about the Tarot may gasp with dismay when the card Death is drawn for their reading, assuming it means the worst. But the Tarot reader will at once assure them that this ominous looking card, with its sinister, skeletal scythe-bearer, does not necessarily mean they should start planning their own funeral. It is a sign of something ending, but this could just as easily be a bad relationship, an unsatisfying job or a period of ill-health. A lot depends on the cards nearby. So with Flight, which can just as easily be a good omen. This symbol means swift change, as its slight resemblance to a zigzag bolt of lightning indicates. Things will change quickly, but they may not be for the worse; in fact this Witchstone speaks of new beginnings, of a changed way of life and a new way of looking at things. The old life is over; the new one has just begun. If this Witchstone appears as the Scythe, its meaning is just the same – the keen blade is about to slice through old ways, old customs, old certainties, and the harvested grain may fall one way or the other...who knows? The keynote with this rune is suddenness, the abrupt change – without warning - from one set of circumstances to another. A 'bolt from the blue' is a good way of thinking of it, a bolt which can be a dire happening or a brilliant inspiration or a massive win on the Pools! A look at Witchstones nearby will give an indication of which way the fortune might fall.

Man

The arrow on the astrological symbol for Mars or an upstanding male member, you can take this symbol as either. Is it a weapon, such as an arrow or spear? If it is, the symbol goes back to our very earliest ancestors at the dawn of time, to *Homo habilis* around two and a half million years ago. Whatever the division of labour then, hunting and weapons have usually been associated since with the male sex. Warfare and hunting both belong to the world of the male, despite 21st century equality and girl army recruits. The soldier, the archer is a male, says the default setting. Cartoon cavemen come home and dump a mammoth on the cave floor in front of their mate, who has been home all day sweeping the cave and sewing skins to make clothing. The symbol thus also conjures up the whole concept of 'bringing home the bacon', as an exclusively male preserve. Thus, as we see, the Man Witchstone cannot speak of female persons. If you didn't like the sexual imagery of the arrow, you could very well use a simple stick figure of a man. This is the male stranger or the male friend or enemy who comes into your life to make a change, to disrupt or lend support.

Woman

Again we have sexual imagery, though more acceptable to modern eyes. The nude female is an object of beauty, encountered in oil paintings and sculptures of enormous worth and artistic merit; where the nude male is usually seen as either deeply shocking or in some way humorous, rather than alluring. This symbol, the triangular shape of a woman's pudenda and thighs, speaks of the physicality of woman, her passivity and receptiveness, her gentleness and nurturing, as against the man's aggressive invasiveness. Passive she may be, but this symbol also speaks of her power. I am reminded of the joke about the little girl, comparing anatomy behind the garden shed with the little boy next door. 'You haven't got one of these,' says the boy, full of male self-satisfaction. 'Doesn't matter,' says the girl, 'my mum says if I've got one of these, I can always get one of those.' Of course there is more to woman's power than her power to attract, but you get the idea.

Again, if you find it objectionable in any way, a simple stick figure could be drawn in a skirt or with long hair.

Star

In almost all cultures the stars are symbols of heaven, of a goal to aim for, a bright future for those who work hard. Many cultures have seen them as sapient beings in their own right, spirits of the sky or masters of our destiny. The stars dictate, through astrology and their influence on the earth, who may attain their desires and who may not. A wondrous star hung over the stable at Nazareth, guiding the Wise Men and appearing at the top of the Christmas tree and in the imagery of much-loved carols ever since. Stars appear universally in heraldry, on many national flags, coins, stamps and commercial emblems. Wicca has a special place for the five-pointed star, which has become a universal symbol of Goddess-based pagan worship.

Think about the word 'star' and its associations in our culture. In the 21st century the worship of celebrity has superseded that of gods or saints in many ways; the star or superstar, the celebrity, is someone whose importance to their fans makes them seem super-human, even when the less-than-super details of their private lives are being revealed. Starlight and stardust are terms we use when we are talking about dreams of success, and the fact that stars are seen only at night does not seem to give them the slightest glimmer of darkness or ill-omen. On the contrary, our grandfathers walked home by starlight and were thankful for it as for a magical aid. The dusk, when the stars start to come out, is seen as a magical time of romantic promise, even though it foretells the later darkness. People speak of 'reaching for the stars' or 'shooting for the stars' when they talk about great ambitions, perhaps ones that can never be achieved. Even a 'falling star' has powers if you see it or can catch it. You may wish upon a star. You may address someone who has done something wonderful for you as 'an absolute star'. Companies give a star rating, and teacher gives a gold star to her star pupils. To me that gold star sums up what this rune is about: achievement and recognition, acclaim, award, prize.

Romance

I feel this symbol suffers from a lack of associated symbolism; perhaps it would be better if drawn as a heart. In fact its lack of subconscious associations (in our culture, at least) are a serious drawback and the reason I finally omitted it from my own set of Witchstones. Clearly it is a sexual symbol of sorts, alluding to the male's erect penis and testes, as well as to the vesica pisces shape (it forms three of these) associated with the female genital anatomy. It looks a little like the triquetra, a little like the Manx triskelion and brings to mind Celtic knot work, none of which have much relation to its given meaning. And this is really all it has to offer us visually.

Eye

One of the one magnetic and powerful images of all is the eye, which evokes an emotional and physical response when it is seen – 'someone is watching you'. The Ancient Egyptians, who also used the eye symbol extensively in their religious imagery, saw it as the seat of consciousness. The god Horus lost his eye when he fought with his wicked uncle Set, to avenge the murder of his father Osiris (who has an eye as part of his written name); in Norse myth Odin also sacrificed his eye to gain knowledge. In both these stories the gods concerned are sun or sky gods, so the one eye is an obvious sun symbol. Greek fishermen paint it on the sides of their boats, so the vessel can 'see where it is going'. In Turkey many people carry the little blue bead known as nazar boncuk, an eye amulet to ward off bad luck. The eye appears in imagery everywhere as a symbol of mystery and knowledge. As the Eye of Providence or Eye of God, the Freemasons use it and it appears on the US $1 bill.

All sorts of mysterious powers are ascribed to the eye, from the evil eye with which a witch or wizard can bring misfortune to their victim (in some African cultures this can happen entirely without the will of the witch) to the dreadful powers possessed by mythical beasts like the basilisk and the gorgon Medusa.

In an age when no street or shopping mall is without its hidden cameras, the eye has taken on a new meaning. 'Eye in the sky' is applied to helicopters monitoring traffic.

The eye is seen as the centre of the person it belongs to, or of an object that has a decided centre; the eye of the storm, the eye of the wind, the eye of a needle. The power of the eye as symbol can also be seen in the way many oil portraits have been painted so that the eyes of the subject follow the viewer around as he moves, whether or not this was deliberate on the part of the artist. Liars or people who have wronged you in some way are supposed not to be able to look you in the eye; those who despise you might spit in your eye. In old belief the eyes of a murdered man would reflect the last image he saw – that of his murderer.

In English, the most widely-spoken language in the world, the word 'eye' is a homophone for 'I', and this is one of the uses of this rune. It represents the querent.

I hope you found all the above stream-of-consciousness interesting and helpful. I hope that you will take it just as a starting point for your own meditations on the symbols, that it has shown you the way but only gone part of the journey with you.

4. Getting Started

Your first step is to acquire a set of witchstones, and there are two obvious ways of doing this. When a witch sets out to acquire a new tool, her first choice should be to consider whether she could make it herself, which will make the tool much more special in a number of ways. If a witch has taken the trouble to go out into the countryside and select a tree, meditated beneath that tree and shared herself with it in some way, the wand she makes from the wood of that tree will be much more efficient and personalised a tool than a wand she bought on eBay with a few clicks of her mouse. It may also save her money!

Of course, it isn't always possible to make all one's tools, and often one does have to go shopping for items in magic shops, whether they are online or in Glastonbury High Street. Some very beautiful items can be bought this way, and they can be consecrated to one's own use. One must also bear in mind the likelihood that the item, bought from a metaphysical shop and probably crafted by someone with at least a working knowledge of magic and ritual, should have been created with the right mental attitudes and even blessed, ready for use. But isn't it a bit like buying chain store clothes when you are a good dressmaker with a sewing machine? If you are anything like me, every garment has to be altered when it comes home from the shop, because it is too tight across the bust, or I decide I don't like the way it buttons at the neck. How much nicer to be able to design and make everything you need, which then has the added advantage of being unique – you will never turn up at a party wearing the same dress as another woman - or at a ritual carrying the same wand as another witch.

It is possible to buy beautiful sets of rune stones on the Net. Some are made of semi-precious stones – I have even found some made from natural, bark-on wood slices - and come ready inscribed with the symbols in a pretty bag with a set of instructions. I can see some of you readers shaking your heads already. It's a bit like having someone follow you around while you enjoy a day out and take all the photographs for you, isn't it? You get the photographs, but if you are anything like me, you want to take your own and decide what you are going to snap, from what angles and how many shots. Why should they have all the fun when it's your camera? The Craft of the Wise is not meant to be easy; it is not something you can buy ready-made at the supermarket.

So I have this advice: do at least try to make your own. What's the worst that can happen? You end up with a set that is less than perfect, but is more meaningful to you than a gleaming set made on a machine and bought from an anonymous Internet seller. Or your attempt ends up in the dustbin – but as you are hopefully using natural materials you have gathered yourself, the cost should be minimal and the trouble put down to experience.

But if you have no artistic ability at all – which I have sympathy with, as there are plenty of things I can't do - you may have to buy your Witchstones, unless you are lucky enough to be given a set, as my magical mentor was given hers by the High Priest who initiated her to Third Degree, and his partner and High Priestess.

Buying your Witchstones: The runes are not readily available everywhere, and you may find you have to buy them from a USA site and wait the extra delivery time. Go online, type 'witch's runestones' into your search engine and select 'Images'. You will see an enormous number of images of Futhark rune sets, and among them, if you are lucky and look carefully, there should be one or two sets of the Witchstones described in this book, though you may have very little choice and they may be quite expensive. You will need to decide whether you want the set of eight or the set of 13, and whether you want costly gemstones, simple pebbles or wooden ones, assuming these are all available.

My own feeling is that wooden ones are nicer – and less likely to chip when thrown a little too enthusiastically. You may feel differently.

Magic and Pagan shops are now everywhere (Goddess be thanked by all busy witches everywhere); you might even find one in your High Street. If you are fortunate enough to live within driving distance of a destination such as Glastonbury or Boscastle, you will be able to explore the shops there, and doubtless find all sorts of treasures to help you in your magical life. Many of these outlets will also do mail order, which will be helpful if you do not live anywhere near such shops. But you may find it difficult describing what you want to a shop assistant on the telephone, so be careful you do not end up with a set of Futhark runes.

If a situation arises where you feel you might pay a little less for a set of stones, the rule is that you don't haggle. You should always pay a fair price for magical items, with no argument. If something is overpriced or beyond your budget, don't buy it (you could always have another go at making your own!).

My last piece of advice is the most important: take your time! Don't click your mouse in a hurry on the first set you see online, thinking, "They'll do". Because they won't, necessarily. As with all magical tools you have to feel drawn to them; they have to feel right. If there's nothing in the marketplace that you feel drawn to, try again another day. You will be glad you did, when you have your perfect set of Witchstones.

In the next chapter I will discuss a few ideas for making your own set, which will hopefully get you enthusiastic about the task, even if you have never done anything like it before. Who knows what other adventures this simple job of painting or carving may lead you on to? It's always useful to be able to use your hands in witchcraft – there's more than one reason it's called the Craft!

5. Making your Witchstones

I wrote earlier that handling your divination tools is a spiritual pleasure in itself - how much more so if you have been able to make your tools yourself. Wicca teaches that making your own tools empowers you; that an athame (a witch's ritual knife) made from metal and wood that you have shaped with your own hands, or even just inscribed yourself, is better than the smartest-looking dagger bought from a store. My own athame was bought online because I have no ability with metalwork, but I have personalised it by decorating it with beads. This was partly done, I admit, because it is an athame that is likely to turn up at rituals with other people who used the same Internet site to order theirs – and it is so easy to pick up the wrong knife when they look the same. But all witches try to personalise their own tools because their tools are a part of them, a part of who they are.

Materials to Make the Witchstones

You can use just about anything to make your Witchstones. I have even seen instructions on an Internet video on YouTube for making runes - in this case they were Futhark runes – from dried butterbeans (lima beans), marking the symbols with a fine-tipped permanent marker. Why not give this a try? As the proud possessor of a jar of baking beans dating from when I was first married 35 years ago, I can tell you they are as likely to last as many other media, and could be a good practice set for you to make.

Small round pebbles make beautiful Witchstones, and are easily acquired on a trip to the beach or a shingly beauty spot. There are few pleasures to compare with wandering along the beach, just above the water-line on a sunny day, with your eyes cast down and your mind in neutral. All sorts of treasures can be found, but especially pretty, smooth round pebbles in a variety of pleasing colours and shapes. Pick up stones as you go, handling each one and looking at it carefully to see if it feels nice in your hand and appeals to you visually. Look for texture, colour, weight and sparkle, bearing in mind that when varnished they will look as they do now when wet (if they are dry dip them in the sea to see what this will be like). Take your time. Size matters! Don't collect pebbles so large that they won't all fit in your hand for a cast. Small bird egg size is probably best, and try to ensure the pebbles are as uniform as possible and also flattish, so that they have a clear 'face' and 'back', and land squarely on one or the other when cast.

The most important thing is that they appeal to you, that you are drawn to them. Don't keep any stones you consider ugly or an unappealing colour. These are for you, a present from you to you, and they should be lovely.

If you can't get to a stony beach or pebbly beauty spot, why not pay a visit to your local garden centre, where small bags of decorative pebbles are often sold inexpensively? Those bluish chippings of slate, for example, would make a very fine base for a set of Witchstones. Or you might even find some likely stones on your own driveway or garden.

You may well find, among the pebbles on the beach, a substance I used to call 'sea-glass' and collect avidly when I was a child. These prettiest of beach gems are actually small pieces of glass from broken bottles that have been tumbled by the sea until they have become smooth, rounded and deliciously frosted. The glass is often a delicate pale blue-green, which may reflect the number of old fashioned ginger beer bottles dropped on the beach by our grandparents in the days before littering was considered so anti-social. Sea-glass is much harder to find nowadays, and when it is, it is often the less attractive green of Beaujolais or beer bottles. But if you do manage to find enough pieces of the right shape and size, they would certainly make very beautiful Witchstones.

Now that the craft of beadwork is so popular, and bead shops are opening in every High Street, it is easy to find plastic, wooden, ceramic or glass beads in a number of shapes, sizes and colours, and these could also be used. Again, choose beads that are flattish, so that they fall on one side or the other, rather than spherical ones. This medium would have the advantage that you could keep your Witchstones on a string and even wear it as a very unusual necklace!

I know someone who makes runes (Futhark in this case) from bone. He buys ordinary cow leg bones from the butcher, the kind sold for dogs, and cleans them by boiling them up in a large saucepan with some ordinary washing powder until they are gleaming white. Then he uses a hacksaw to cut them lengthways several times until he has long sticks of bone, then across into small squares. These squares must then be filed on one side to smooth away the labyrinthine structures which were on the inside of the bone. Once polished, the bone squares, now looking just like ivory, can be incised with the symbols, and he then smears boot polish on to the surface and rubs it into the marks to make them show up clearly. This is obviously a long process, but at the end of it you would have a set of Witchstones that you had made yourself from scratch. This option might not sit well with a vegetarian, but the material would surely be more acceptable than real ivory, considering that the animal was killed for food instead of just for its tusks.

If you aren't worried about the cost and wish to treat yourself to the most magnificent set money can buy, why not pay a visit to the local crystal shop and browse their small crystal baskets? Some crystals are sold at a few pence each, though many are pounds apiece. It may be difficult to find enough pieces of a uniform shape, but a word with the manager may help, as he or she may have a contact who could produce uniform pieces to order (don't worry – most crystal shop staff are well accustomed to the needs of Pagan customers, and will not be fazed by your inquiry or regard you as some kind of weirdo). Choose pieces that are made from the same type of crystal, and choose a crystal that you are drawn to, so that if you reach to pick up another type, your hand wavers and moves almost of its own volition to the right ones. This tells you that this is the crystal you should go for. I hope it isn't the most expensive one!

Wood is an excellent option because it can be easily acquired, then shaped, sanded, painted or carved, and varnished. Small discs cut from a length of wooden dowel, such as an old curtain pole or broomstick, can be sanded smooth – a sensuous experience in itself – and made as uniform as possible. Or you could find an old branch (please do not cut one from a living tree unless you have to, and then be sure you ask the tree's permission and leave an offering for it afterwards, such as a lock of your hair or a small coin. A drink of water with some plant feed might be appreciated, too). Cut the branch into discs. A pleasing effect is achieved if you leave the bark on, but you can peel it off if you prefer. The piece of wood should be between two and four centimetres in diameter, and as round in section as possible. Use a fine-toothed saw to cut the pieces probably no thicker than half a centimetre.

It is also quite easy to make square Witchstones from a narrow plank of wood (perhaps 1inch or 3cm wide) by cutting off square pieces and sanding them smooth. You can also take off the corners and the hard edges with the sandpaper to give a pleasing cushion or cake-of-soap shape. The possibilities are only limited by your imagination.

If the wood is green – not seasoned or aged – it should now be left somewhere warm and dry for a few days to allow the sap to dry.

When the wood seems dry you can start to apply the artwork, using whatever method seems good to you. If you wish, you can draw the design on lightly with a soft pencil before applying the permanent design.

Clay or modelling clay is also a very good medium, and this is the only substance I would cheerfully have a go at carving, or inscribing. If you can make uniform clay tablets, round or square as you prefer, and then have them fired, they would be ideal. If you didn't want to inscribe them before firing, they could be painted afterwards, or you could paint into the inscribed detail to enhance it. Some modelling clays now available are air-hardening - although their fibrous nature means they are not quite so easy to use as natural clay - and these could be ideal for your Witchstones, and can be painted and varnished once they are dry. Have a look and see what is available in your nearest hobby shop.

If you have never used clay or plasticine in your life, I can assure you that making little tablets couldn't be easier. Divide up the material into equal-sized balls, about the size of a hazelnut (filbert), then take each ball and carefully squash it with your thumb on a flat surface until you have made it into a tablet, round or oval. The back of a dessert spoon can be used gently to help with the shaping. Turn it over and press gently again, to make sure both sides are flat. If the clay cracks around the edges, smooth it with your fingers and a little water.

Can I suggest that you create quite a few more discs or squares than you will actually need? Even if you do not throw away a few that did not turn out as desired, you should have some in reserve for when you decide to expand your set of runes.

Creating the Designs

Anyone who has any ability at carving could certainly have a go at this, but for most people I wouldn't recommend it, as it would probably be a recipe for disaster and gashed fingers. If you own a very sharp craft knife you could carve the designs in lightly, then smear some pigment, such as boot-black, into the scratches to make them stand out.

Painting on wood, beads or stones alike should be simple if you ensure the Witchstones are lovely and clean, completely free of grease, and as flat as possible on the surface you wish to paint the design on. Tumbled crystals or beach pebbles already have a 'key' from their polishing, and should take the paint and varnish well, and wood is the most suitable of all for painting.

For the round shapes, such as the Rings and the Sun, you could use a very small bottle lid, a small shirt button, small coin or the head of a drawing pin to draw round, or you could trace the shapes on to the wood using the old nursery school skill of two-sided tracing. Trace the design on one side, then turn the tracing paper over and trace the design as you can see it through the tracing paper. Now turn it over again, lay it on the piece to be decorated, and re-trace the first design, using pressure to transfer the pencil mark to the piece of wood. This won't work as well for stone, but you could give it a try.

Use a very fine brush – eyeliner brushes are very good for this - and poster paint or modelling enamel to create the design, making it as simple or elaborate as you wish. If you make a mistake, don't despair. Remove the paint quickly, if it is still wet, with water if using poster paint or white spirit if using enamel. Or with wood the piece can be left until it is quite dry, then the mistake can be sanded off and you can start again. When it is finished to your satisfaction, leave it to dry overnight.

You may find, with some more absorbent woods, that the paint sinks in very quickly and then seeps, leaving a nasty fluffy line instead of the crisp, clean lines you want. This is easily prevented by coating the surface of the wood with a thin coat of the varnish you will use later to seal them. When this is dry, you can paint on the top of it, and there should be no problems.

If you find using a fine paintbrush difficult, you could also use a permanent marker pen, such as a Sharpie®; as these come in a range of colours you could create some very pretty Witchstones.

The back of the Witchstones can be left plain, or you can decorate them all with the same design, such as your own runic signature or just a decorative squiggle. Be sure not to make this too large or elaborate, as you will need to see at a glance which Witchstones have landed face-up and which face-down when you make a cast.

If you like, wooden Witchstones can be decorated with pokerwork, using a hot soldering iron and a lot of care. On a paler wood this can look truly stunning, and the fresh, informal nature of this art means the drawing doesn't have to be 100 per cent precise. I have a lovely wooden chopping board in my kitchen that my husband would insist on using to slice cake on, even though I keep it for onions. So I decorated it with a picture of an onion to show what it was for, using a soldering iron borrowed from my husband's tool drawer. It is surprisingly easy to do. It would be a good idea to wear some heatproof gloves to do this; if you do not have any, wear two pairs of washing-up gloves, or fine gardening gloves would at least provide some protection if you happened to touch the hot end by accident. The rules are: don't lay it down on a polished or other delicate surface, don't leave it where children or animals can get at it, and do leave it to cool before you put it back.

Use the tip of the soldering iron exactly as you would a pen nib, marking the wood very slowly until you have the depth of brown you want. I find it is best to keep the iron moving back and forth along the line in a small 'scribbling' movement, to avoid a blobby 'join-up-the-dots' look. Then varnish the runes as before. The disadvantage of this method is that if you do make a mistake, the burn may go quite a depth into the wood, making it difficult to sand it away.

If you really don't feel confident doing any of these things, why not try the traditional art of decoupage? This sounds a bit scary, but is easy as anything. Find some tiny pictures of the symbols you want to use – and this will be the hardest part, I assure you – cut them out, either close to their outline or with a small area of the surrounding paper left around them – and stick them on the Witchstones with glue. You might even find small transfers you could use. If you are better with paper than with wood or stone, you could create the artwork yourself on paper, then cut it out and use it. Let it dry thoroughly.

Making your Witchstones

Now that your designs are finished, varnish the Witchstones, using either an acrylic varnish applied with a brush, or a clear spray lacquer, and making sure you protect your tabletop with plenty of newspaper before you start. The water-based acrylic varnishes and the spray lacquers dry very quickly, but they should be left a couple of hours before you apply another coat, and overnight before you turn them over to varnish the other side. If you can balance the stones on top of a small bottle lid or cotton reel, this should stop the varnish running down and sticking them to the newspaper as they dry. Always apply the varnish thinly, if you are using a brush; if you get drip marks underneath despite your care, wait until they are completely dry and sand them off carefully with fine sandpaper.

Varnishing the stones is important because not only does it protect the artwork, but it enhances the symbols and the colours you have used. If you are really into "bling" and want your Witchstones to look really glitzy, you could make one of the coats glitter spray paint – a clear lacquer with silver or gold glitter in it. Do not make this the top coat, as in my experience it can rub off.

You may also want to make a small drawstring bag to keep your stones in. This is very quickly run up on the sewing machine from any piece of fabric you may have in the rag-bag. I would suggest a fairly stiff fabric such as can be cut from old jeans or corduroy trousers (if you cut a section from the narrow part of the leg, it will save you a lot of sewing), which will protect the stones and is unlikely to wear into holes. If you find making a drawstring bag too difficult to even think about, make a satchel-shaped bag and sew a row of poppers to the flap and front of the bag to fasten it securely. Or make a simple bag and just wind a cord around the top and knot it to keep the contents secure.

If you are an utter klutz with a needle, you can always buy a small bag or use a bag in which gift toiletries, sweets or other goodies were given, or even a soft zipper-fastened pencil case – they come in all colours and finishes from denim to bright pink fur. If you are happy with it, that's all that matters.

And now your very own Witchstones, unique to you, are ready to consecrate and use.

6. Using your Witchstones

Stones O'Leary, Stones O'Leary
Tell me truly, tell me clearly
Give to me an answer true
Show me what I am to do
Let my eye see clear and bright
That I may see my future right.

I have heard it said that the old Celtic sea-god Llyr or Lir is the O'Leary referred to in this rhyme. Whether he is or not, no doubt our ancestors at some point attributed the Witchstones to some deity, just as gods often get the credit for alphabets such as the Egyptian hieroglyphs and the Norse runes. But whoever invented them, this is a pleasant little rhyme to focus your mind as you prepare to cast them.

You may wish to consecrate your runes. Any simple ceremony you can devise which pleases you is fine for this. A Wiccan would start by casting a circle, but this book is not intended as a general Wiccan handbook, so I will not go into all that. There are plenty of other books on the market that will give detailed instructions for this. If you are interested in Wicca, you probably already have some of them. If you are not, I don't see that performing a ritual that is meaningless to you will help you use and develop a relationship with your Witchstones.

A very simple way to 'clean' and consecrate your runes is to sprinkle them with salt water. Take a small cup or bowl of plain water and a small saucer or dish of salt (a pinch is enough), and ask whatever deity you believe in to bless and purify these substances. Plain tap water and cooking salt are fine, but you can also use water taken from Chalice Well at Glastonbury, or any other holy well, or sea water, with the most expensive sea salt you can find, if you like. Dip your finger into each one, strongly imagining all negative energies fleeing away out of them and into the ground as you do so. Tip the salt into the water and stir clockwise a few times to dissolve. Sprinkle the salted water over the Witchstones (you can wipe them afterwards), imagining as you do all the negative energies flowing out of them – try visualising this as dark smoke, flowing away into the ground. This is important if the materials you are using are not new – think of the bad energies an old curtain pole, from which you might have cut discs for your set, could collect in a house where the owners are always quarrelling.

In my experience not many people are able to come up with ritual words on an ad hoc basis, so you may like to use the following words, or write your own.

> '*Goddess (or whoever you wish to invoke), I ask your blessing on these Witchstones, that they may become a useful tool to me on my magical path. Let them speak to me and let me hear and understand them, between the worlds and in all the worlds.*'

You may also wish to present your Witchstones to the four elements. Put your Witchstones in a small basket or a bag so they may all be picked up together – a clean paper bag (not plastic) will do, if you haven't yet made a proper pouch for them, or place them in a string net of the kind used for oranges or onions. Have a candle and incense or joss sticks on the table, together with either a crystal, a dish of soil or a stone from the garden. Pass your witchstones through the incense smoke and ask the Lords of Air to bless them, using the same format as before. Do the same with the candle flame (quickly and carefully!), addressing the Lords of Fire, and finally touching the witchstones to the crystal, soil or stone and asking the Lords of Earth for their blessing. You have already presented them to the element of Water by sprinkling them with the salted water.

If you are a Christian, or belong to some other faith which does not recognise the elements, you can simply pray for your stones, that they become a useful tool for you.

A Wiccan might feel inclined to take all this a step further, and anoint them with her blood, but there is no need for you to do this if you shudder at the thought. The Witchstones will take on your energies simply from being owned by you, and still more if you carry them often with you, or keep them next to your bed. Handle them often, stroke them and look at them. Do not let others touch them without your express permission. If all this seems nonsensical to you, think of psychometrists, who can tell you all about the owner of an object, someone perhaps many years dead, just by touching something that once belonged to them.

Doodle with your Witchstones: if you are a doodler, you can sit and do this at work and no one will notice or think anything of it. Use the witchstone you are 'imprinting' at the time. Perhaps it is the Sun: when you are doodling, draw little suns all over the corner of the page. It is a good way of keeping the image in the front of your mind.

Record your dreams: while you are charging your Witchstones with your own energies, you will have them at your bedside – perhaps they will be the last thing you look at before you sleep. Keep a notebook by your bed, and write down any dreams you remember on waking. Examine the dreams carefully for images related to the symbols on your stones. Record these with the daily reading of your Witchstones to see what the day will bring.

Here is a simple little exercise which will help you 'imprint' your runes with your own energies: pile the runes up in a heap that will be easy to pick up in one go. Rub your palms together gently to start your energies working, then move them apart. Bring your palms together slowly until you can feel the energies as a kind of warm 'ball' between your hands. Concentrate on this for a moment, encouraging the feeling to grow, then place your hands around the Witchstones and hold them there, sending your energies into them. Do this as often as you like to imbue the Witchstones with your psychic energy.

If you expand your system and add more Witchstones, consecrate them in the manner described above before adding them to the set.

Consecrate a small notebook bought specially for this purpose for use with your Witchstones, and start each session by writing the date, the situation you are experiencing and the question you want to ask in the notebook. Then, when you have cast the Witchstones, carefully draw a little map of how they fall, with each one named or identified by its own symbol. It is very interesting to have a record of what the Witchstones tell you, so that you can look back at it later, and see how accurate the cast was in the light of later events, and this simple exercise, if carried out regularly, will be invaluable in helping you to develop an ever deeper understanding of what your runes tell you. It is a learning process; the stones do not always have just one meaning, and if you can compare a cast with the outcome it will help with learning alternative meanings and deeper levels of meaning.

Now you are ready to begin.

Having spent so much time creating your Witchstones, you may want to have a soft cloth or a small mat to cast the stones upon so they do not get scratched. Take your time about this, as you did with the Witchstones themselves. Choose or make something that gives you pleasure. If you are very clever with a needle, you may be able to make a casting cloth that folds up and becomes the carrying pouch.

When you are ready to do a reading, sit down and ground and centre yourself. There are many ways of doing this, but the one I generally use is this: sit as comfortably as possible in a chair or on the ground. Close your eyes and take a deep breath, into your belly. Push the lowest part of your tummy right out to pull in as much air as possible (don't worry – no one's looking but the Goddess!). Feel the volume of air smoothing and soothing within you, ironing out creases and cramps. Enjoy the feeling. Then puff the air out again, making a huffing sound if you feel you want to, and seeing all your stress and tension going out of you with the breath. Imagine this as black smoke, pouring out of you. Do this at least twice more, then you should feel a great deal more relaxed; some people will actually sense the pattern of their thoughts slowing and changing in intensity.

Now, still with your eyes closed, imagine roots growing out of your base, or a rope being let down from your base into the chair and through the chair into the ground. Down and down it goes, until it hooks around a big rock at the earth's centre. Take some more deep breaths – always into your belly, not your chest – and puff out stress and negativity as before.

If you are a little more experienced, perhaps a practising Wiccan, you may want to open your chakras now, but if you have no idea what this means, it does not matter; there are other ways of achieving the receptive stillness which is the best mental posture for casting the stones. Allow your mind to become still. Listen to your breathing and notice the sensation of your breath under your nose; allow this to fill your head until all other thoughts drift away and you become still and peaceful.

Simple Casting

The first step is to think carefully about your question. It may be that you just want a general reading for the day: what will today bring me? Or you may have a specific question about some area of your life that is troubling you or puzzling you at the present time. Think carefully about how you phrase this question. 'Is my boss about to sack me?' might be the question that is running through your mind, but does not leave the witchstones much leeway for giving you a message, and also leaves no room for any further information, whether the answer is 'yes, he is' or 'no, he isn't'. Try instead a general question about your career and work situation, such as 'What is going on with my career?' It could be that Mr Roberts has indeed got your P45 in his in-tray, but another job opportunity is coming your way which will vastly improve your situation and make you glad you left the old, unsatisfactory position.

Take out the Eye and lay it centrally on the casting cloth – this will be the focus of your reading. Take the Witchstones into your hands and hold them while you concentrate on the question you want to ask. Still concentrating on your question and on the witchstones and the link between the two, softly cast the stones like dice upon the cloth.

Some Witchstones will have fallen face down; remove these and place them back in their bag. They have no message for you this time. The only exception to this is where a stone has fallen face-down over the Eye itself. In this case I would look at the reversed Witchstone just to see what it was, and then read it as a sort of 'ghost' with the others, its meaning very diluted (if all the witchstones have fallen face down, there is no answer for you today. Put them away, thank the Goddess and return to them another day for a reading).

At this stage you may want to record the cast in your notebook, writing the date and your question at the top of the page. Make a little map of how the stones fell, and label each one with its symbol or name.

With the Futhark runes any stones that have fallen upside-down, that is with their symbol reversed, have a different meaning from those which have fallen facing towards you; however this is not the case with the Witchstones, many of which are fairly symmetrical in any case.

Take the Eye as the starting point, and note the first rune, which is that nearest to the Eye – it may even be lying across the Eye stone. This is the one most relevant to your answer, or the one that will come true earliest; those further away are less relevant or immediate. Any stones not landing on the cloth should be discarded as not relevant. Stones that fall very close together or lie one on top of another have a combined meaning, even if they do not immediately seem compatible. If any stones have fallen in a special way, such as leaning together, make a note of this. Follow the path out from the Eye, noting all the stones in order of closeness to the Eye. I prefer to do this in a clockwise spiral, as if the Eye were at the centre of the spiral. When I am doing readings for other people not present, I sometimes use the Eye as the centre of the cast but lay it face down before I start.

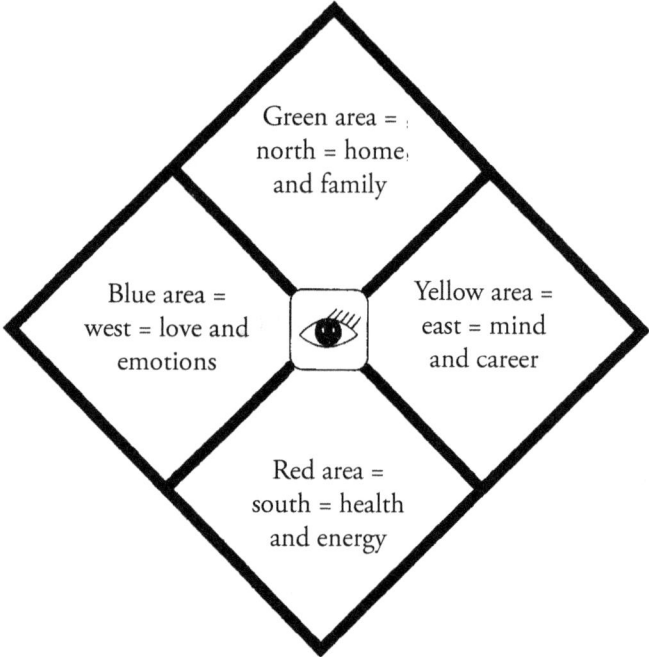

Green area =
north = home
and family

Blue area =
west = love and
emotions

Yellow area =
east = mind
and career

Red area =
south = health
and energy

Element Casting

Those who have more experience of working with the elements may wish to do a cast based on them. For this you will need a cloth or sheet of paper divided into four or five.

Four Elements

If you wish, you can make up a casting cloth of four squares of coloured material, made up to represent the four elements. The coloured pieces should be stitched together thus: top left green, top right yellow, bottom left blue, bottom right red. If you then rotate the cloth 45 degrees into a diamond shape, you will have green at the top, yellow at the right, red at the bottom and blue on the left. These represent the cardinal points north (green), east (yellow), south (red) and west (blue). In an ideal world, you would also have ascertained where the cardinal points lie and laid out your cloth in the correct alignment, with north at north. You can buy a small key-ring-sized compass to go with your set, if you wish to do this. In Wicca these elements have their own territories and areas of influence – for which see the correspondences given in chapter two. For casting purposes we now take these areas to mean our home (north, green), the mind, i.e. our working life and career (east, yellow), our health (south, red) and our emotional life, i.e. our love life (west, blue).

Place the Eye on the centre point where the four colours meet, and cast the witchstones around it. The square on which a Witchstone falls then tells you about which area of your life it has a message.

Five Elements

Wiccans would add a fifth element to the four, that of spirit, which is coloured purple. If you wanted to add this element, I would suggest you could add a wide purple border to the casting cloth, or stitch a broad purple cross into the cloth to divide up the other four colours. Witchstones that fall on this purple area would then speak of your spiritual life and progress.

Layouts

Witchstones may also be drawn from the bag and laid face down in the same manner as Tarot cards, and there are a number of ways to do this. The very simplest one is of course to draw one runestone for a simple answer which might be just 'yes' or 'no'. Put your hand into the bag and turn the Witchstones over between your fingers (without looking into the bag), concentrating as you do so on the question in your mind. As you touch the stones you will eventually find one that wants to be in your fingers; perhaps it will just 'pop' into your hand, or it may feel warm and even tingle in your hand. This is the one with a message for you. Draw it out and look at it.

With the drawing of one, if the message puzzles you, you may ask the Witchstones to clarify. Say 'clarify, please' and draw another in the same way. Do not do this more than once; it is disrespectful and will harm the relationship you are building with the Witchstones.

The next simplest is the layout of three, which represents past, present and future. The first rune shows you how you have come to this situation, the middle one tells you the situation you are in and the third tells you of the path ahead. Again, you may ask for clarification if you cannot understand the message, but you will usually find with hindsight that the message was right.

A set of four may be laid in the same way, representing the distant past, the factors that led to the present, the current situation and the future.

Other layouts include the Wheel of the Year, in which the stones are laid out widdershins (anti-clockwise) in a circle of eight which represent the Wiccan Wheel of the Year, the eight Sabbats spaced through the year. This can be read according to the present time of year, with the runestone that lands on the nearest Sabbat being read as the present situation, and the other Sabbats being taken as rough timescales for the Witchstones which are laid on them.

Element layouts made be made by drawing Witchstones one at a time from the bag and laying them in a diamond, with the north representing your home and family, the east your career, the south your health and the west your romantic life. Or you can lay out five, with the central one representing your spiritual life, or a pentagram (five pointed star) layout, with the five elements, including spirit, represented by the points of the star.

Those of you familiar with the Tarot can also use the spreads recommended by Tarot readers, such as the seven card horseshoe and the Celtic Cross. In the horseshoe the cards are laid out in an arc, and read in the following order: one (first card on your left) is the past, two the present, three is hidden influences, four (the central card) is obstacles, five the surrounding influences or environment, six is what should be done and seven is the outcome.

The Celtic Cross consists of a cross of five cards, one for each direction and one in the middle, with a sixth card laid across it, then a line of four cards laid vertically to the right of the cross. Card one is the card at the centre of the cross, under the card laid over it, and relates to the question and the querent's attitude to it. Two is the card laid over this one and speaks of obstacles in his or her path. Three is the top of the cross, furthest from the reader, and speaks of immediate plans and expected events facing the querent. Four is the bottom card and speaks of past influences with a direct bearing on the situation. Five lies to the right of the centre and is about past influences which are fading away. Six is to the left and speaks of new circumstances arising. Card seven is the bottom of the line of four and is about the querent's state of mind and feelings. Eight is the next one up and speaks of the environment or home life. Nine is the top but one and is about hopes and fears, and ten is the outcome. I won't go into any other Tarot spreads here, because this information is all available on Tarot websites and in books about the subject, which can all give you more information than I have space for here.

So much for my ideas – now how about yours? This book is about finding your own ways, which suit you better than other people's, so why not come up with a layout of your own? Design the layout yourself, according to your own criteria, and firmly stating which position speaks of which set of influences, and you are well on your way to using your own system. You might, for example, like the idea of a circular layout which is read by jumping to opposite Witchstones around the ring. To start with you can draw the circle in your record book, clearly labelling each position with what it represents and referring to this until you know it well enough not to need the book. The possibilities are only limited by your own imagination.

7. Reading the Witchstones

The purpose of this chapter is not to provide a handy little index of exact meanings of every combination of the Witchstones, to save you any trouble or from having to learn to read them for yourself; magic doesn't work like that. Although certain combinations of the Witchstones can certainly point in a certain direction, there is not really a set meaning for any combination, however convincing it may seem (though I have certainly had a disagreement with my mother in the evening after drawing the Crossed Arrows and the Moon that morning, and been whisked out unexpectedly for dinner by my other half after drawing the Star and Romance symbols, and anyone seeing the Birds lying next to the Crossed Arrows would feel justified in expecting some bad news). Each symbol has to be read with reference to those lying nearby, and even how near or far apart they fall has an influence on the reading; also with reference to your own situation and the question you asked before you cast the stones. The symbols are also very likely to be a message for you personally, a message about your spiritual life or path, rather than a specific prediction of some event that is going to befall you. The Powers that rule are not as interested in warning you that you may get a big zit just before your hot date on Friday as they are in advising you that you should take thought for others or give up bad habits in favour of good ones or turn your thoughts to spiritual matters. If you need an answer about some specific area of your life, such as love, career or health, you need to ask the question before making the cast or draw.

With any cast of Witchstones the negative or positive quality of the stones is a very important part of the meaning. Getting the Sun, the Ear of Corn and the Star all together in one cast is certainly going to put a smile on your face, while you might very well think 'ooh-er, this doesn't look good!' if you get the Arrows and the Flight stones lying together. The rule is that the Witchstones influence each other; they should not be read singly if they are clearly lying in close proximity – this indicates a relationship between them. If you see the Arrows lying right next to the Wave, it most probably doesn't mean that you will have a car breakdown one day and then go on holiday the following week; more likely it means your holiday plans will be disrupted by some problem. More likely still it is a message aimed at your spiritual nature, such as the advice that you should expect a revelation about something that has troubled you since your childhood, or that a quick change to old ways and thought patterns dating from childhood or inherited from your parents is needed.

With practice you will soon develop a good eye for summing up the cast at a glance, but you should still go on to carefully record the cast and the positions of all the Witchstones in your notebook. This concentrates the mind, is good practice and also ensures you have a detailed record of your cast to refer back to in the light of future events in your life. As I said, learning the Witchstones is an ongoing process; they will always have something to teach you. And what is close proximity? I will have to leave you to judge that for yourself. Don't sit there with a tape measure, measuring the distance between the Witchstones, but do use your instincts and your common sense.

The Witchstones may also indicate timescales by their distance from the Eye, so if you find a stone that has rolled away and gone under the table a few feet away, but is still face-up, you can take that as meaning that its message refers to something that is some way in the future.

Now let us have a look at some casts and find out what we can learn from them. For these exercises I am using sometimes the traditional set of 13 and sometimes my own personalised set (which is indicated in the text), but you will learn to apply these methods to your own personalised system as you progress in the art. Some of these are taken from my own record of draws and casts made for my own information or for others; some are made up simply as an example.

Cast One

Here the Eye is partly covered by the Moon, which has fallen onto it, with the Flight nearby, almost touching. These three witchstones are the most important and immediate aspect of the cast, though there is another interesting little group nearby, the Ear of Corn, Arrows and the Birds. The Man and the Romance stones are lying singly and further away; these are of less interest, although they should still be recorded and read. The other stones have fallen face-down; they will not be read and can be removed from the casting cloth before the cast is read and recorded.

The group around the Eye could speak of something happening within your family, a sudden change. It is not necessarily something bad, but something unexpected and soon to occur. It could mean your mother; or it could indicate a timescale of

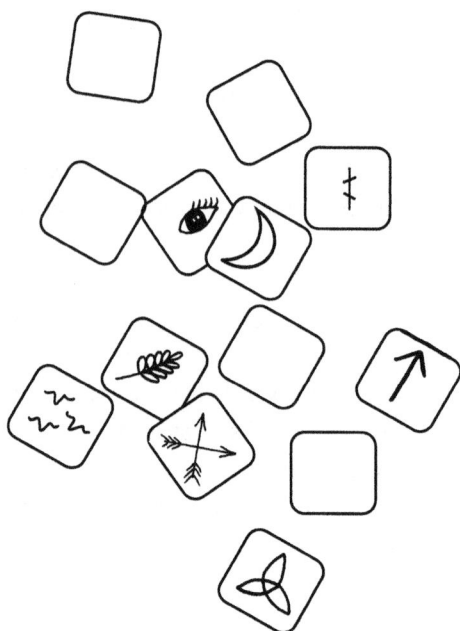

a month. My feeling would be the former, as the Moon is so closely linked to the Eye. Or the Moon laid over the eye in that manner could mean that something interesting will occur within your psychic or spiritual life. Close your eyes and let your mind linger gently on this group of Witchstones, and very likely you will receive some indication of what this could be about. If you don't, don't worry. At this early stage of your relationship with the Witchstones, it is more important to record casts to see what they can teach you.

Now move on to the next group, the Corn, the Arrows and the Birds. The Corn indicates that you will prevail in whatever you are trying to do, but the Arrows show it will not be easy. Hard work and struggle will reach a result that is worth it all, and there could be a piece of news or a surprise in store of a pleasant nature, indicated by the Birds. Although the Arrows is a negative symbol, it lies with the Corn, which is strongly positive, and the Birds, which is mildly positive, so its negativity is weakened.

Cast Two

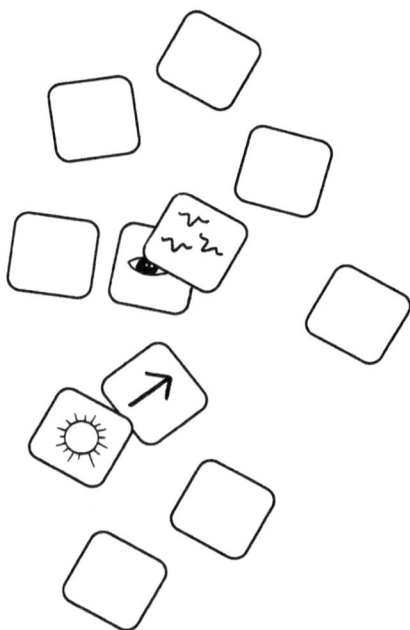

My friend Susan came to me, very concerned about a rumour she had heard that her son-in-law had been cheating on her daughter. He worked in the same office as a not-very-close friend of hers, who had made it her business to pass this gossip on to Susan; some people do enjoy giving other people bad news, don't they? Obviously she had said nothing to her daughter of what she had heard, but she was very upset and worried. She didn't really believe in any of the fortune-telling systems I use, but she needed something to occupy her mind and perhaps make her laugh for a little while, so I offered her a reading of the witchstones. She laughed, and said it would be as good a way of passing the time as any, and she was up for it as long as I didn't expect her to believe in any of 'that nonsense' (I have changed some details here, so that my friend is not in any way identified or made to feel exposed or embarrassed).

I asked her to take the stones into her hands and take time to think about her worries before casting them gently on to the tablecloth. We did not use the Eye as representing the querent, as her question was not about herself.

The Eye, however, thought otherwise. It landed with the Birds perched exactly on top of it – how could this be read other than as a reference to my friend hearing gossip which filled her mind and blinded her to the truth? Most of the Witchstones had landed face down, but a pair of stones gave her answer: the Man and the Sun, which had fallen nearby with their edges touching. The Man represented the son-in-law and the Sun promised light on his deeds and truth; with no negative Witchstone nearby this seemed to indicate that he was guiltless.

A fortnight later she rang me, breathless with relief. Her friend had called her, saying she was sorry to hear that Susan's daughter was now separating from her cheating husband. As Susan knew this was not the case, she probed further and found the woman had mistaken the identity of her son-in-law, and had been telling her about the shenanigans of a younger man with the same first name, working in the same office.

Cast Three

Another friend called on me, quite excited because she had been offered a new job at a better rate of pay. The job called for a little more travel each day, but she didn't mind that. But obviously she had mixed feelings about the position, because she suggested I do

a reading for her to 'see how it would turn out'. I often find non-pagan friends will do this – they say they don't believe in the Witchstones or their messages, but they do still seem to need to see them, perhaps as a way of clarifying their own feelings and instincts, and will ask for a reading 'for fun'.
She laid the Eye and used it as the focus for the casting.

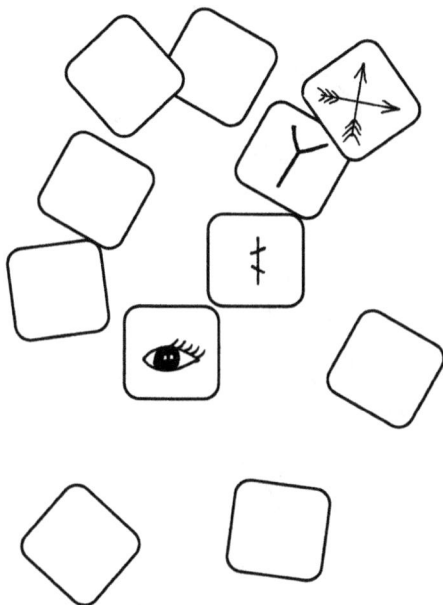

At once we could both see that something bad was indicated. Near the Eye lay the Flight, and very close to that lay the Woman, with the Crossed Arrows slightly on top. My feeling was that this indicated an unpleasant boss or someone else in the new position that would make life difficult for her, but we were not to know the details. She did not take the job, and a few months later she told me it was being advertised again. Had someone else who got the job found the position was difficult or the office manageress impossible to get on with?

Cast Four

Here the Man and the Rings sit very close to the Eye in a reading done for someone female who has asked if they will meet a romantic partner.

All seems very clear, except that the Moon and the Arrows are also very close to these Witchstones. This lady will meet an attractive man, but I would fear from the symbols cast that he might turn out to be a love rat! The Moon is a neutral symbol which can speak of psychic development, but in a situation where someone has asked about romance the Moon can mean betrayal or lies, and the Arrows speak for themselves, telling of an unfortunate encounter; perhaps even violence. Don't give him your phone number, love – plenty more fish in the sea!

Cast Five

I cast this when a close friend was pregnant. She had remarried recently and was now in her forties; although the pregnancy was not her first it had not gone without problems, and I was concerned for her. As you can see, the Crossed Arrows lie atop the reversed Eye – shown as a blank - and the cast seems to lie in a widdershins (anti-clockwise – ill-omened to a Wiccan) spiral. My friend suffered from many antenatal health problems and the birth, which happened a month prematurely, was difficult and dangerous; because the labour was not going well the obstetrician finally decided to perform a Caesarean section. The Flight, lying very close to the Eye and Arrows, indicates a sudden occurrence, in this case the hurried decision to operate following the premature labour and the dangers that went with it. Then the Wheel, my own symbol, showing progress, and finally the Earth (my own symbol, indicating home and safety) and Sun symbols, showing her home, happy and safe with the Stranger (again, my own symbol), clearly her new daughter. The Sun and Earth symbols near the end of the spread clearly show a happy ending.

Cast Six

This cast was made one New Year's Eve, and my question was simply, what will the New Year bring? Because I left it so open, the stones themselves concentrated, as they tend to do, on my spiritual life, rather than whether I was going to meet any tall dark strangers or win the Pools. The Woman sits tipped with its edge on the Eye, with the Lightning (the same meaning as Flight) very close by, and the surrounding stones are the Wheel (my own symbol, speaking of progress), the Rings, the Ear of Corn, the Moon and the Star, the former two speaking of rewarding friendship and the latter two speaking very eloquently of pagan spirituality. Quite early in the ensuing year, and after 20 years as a solitary witch, I met a lady who joined my WI and who turned out to have pagan leanings and to be very interested in Wicca and related subjects. She also introduced another like-minded friend, and the three of us worked happily together as a small coven for some time. Because I had these friends, I was motivated and confident enough to go to pagan moots, and thus met the High Priestess who was to tutor me to proper Gardnerian initiation later on. For all of us, Green Frog Coven was a time of new beginnings and promise which has been fulfilled for all of us. This cast also illustrates the fact that the Lightning or Flight is a neutral symbol – although it speaks of sudden change, that change may as easily be something very beneficial as a sudden death or serious accident.

Cast Seven

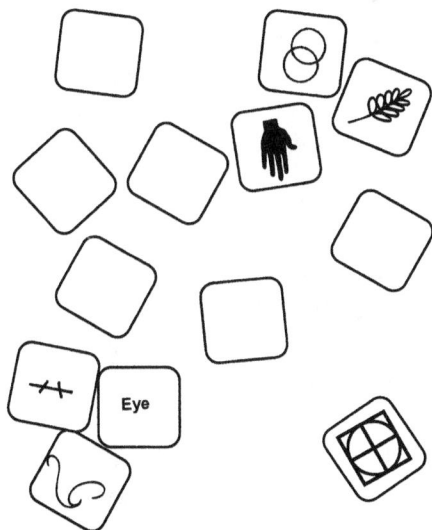

This casting was for a friend whose husband walked out, leaving her with two children, and with minimal confidence for a long time. The Flight and the Wave, both touching the reversed Eye, show him leaving, but a little way off lie the Stranger (my own symbol), the Ear of Corn and the Rings, a clear reference to the lovely man she met about a year later. Still further off is the Earth (my own symbol), which speaks of the home they made together.

I like stories with happy endings!

Cast Eight

This cast is one I made several years ago now, when my husband and I were discussing whether to move home or extend our current house, which had become a little too small for our needs. As you see, the Sun and Moon lie on either side of the Eye, representing him and me and our two viewpoints. Then comes the Flight – a sudden change - and my own symbol the Cup, which speaks of choices. Then comes the Wall, again my own symbol, speaking of blockage. And beyond that the Wave and the Ear of Corn. I read all this to mean that I would get my own way and we would extend (he was the one who wanted to move, whilst I loved my house and wanted to stay there, even if it meant builders on site). The last two Witchstones surely pointed at a well-earned holiday following the work! At this stage, as you can see, I was still not a very skilled reader of the Witchstones, and it also demonstrates that one should not let wishful thinking cloud one's judgement and get in the way of the reading! Looking back, I can see as plain as print that the Flight showed the coming of the factors that made a move inevitable: my widowed mother needed to come and live with us and our village was suddenly threatened with a large development that made us feel we would rather be somewhere else. The choice was only where we would move to, and the blockage turned out to be the hard time we had buying our Cornish cottage, followed by the Wave (move) and Corn (our reward, moving into the home we dreamed of). If I had been better at reading the runes in those times, I would have started packing up my china when I saw this cast.

Cast Nine

Here the Woman sits between the Flight and the Wave. This is a more serious casting, one I have invented for the purposes of this chapter. A man has asked about his wife, diagnosed with cancer, and whether she will get better or whether he has to face losing her. This would be a difficult one for even a very experienced witch or diviner to handle, and my advice to anyone reading Witchstones would be to gently refuse his request but offer any kind of help or healing that you can. The gods do not like answering life and death questions, and those who ask them often do not like the answer, either. What purpose is served by telling this man that the Witchstones indicate that his wife may be going to die? Sufficient unto the day is the evil thereof, and he should be spending his time supporting and caring for his wife and making the most of his time with her, rather than brooding on the fate that awaits. Hope is better than dread, and you would be doing him no favour by giving him the obvious meaning of this spread.

Cast Ten

Right, something a bit more cheerful. This reading was for a neighbour who was puzzled as to whether she should offer financial help to a dear friend who was going through money difficulties, or whether she would risk offending her – what a lovely friend to have when you are down on your luck! The poor friend had lost her job and was struggling to find another position that would pay enough for her to be able to afford a childminder for her little boy, as she was a single mum.

The kind neighbour cast the Witchstones rather clumsily and they all fell in a little heap on the Eye, but they were good stones. Around and on top of the Eye lay a jumble consisting of some reversed Witchstones which I set aside, and the Rings, Woman, Cup (my own symbol, meaning choice), Sun and Harvest. I explained to her that the Rings in this case had nothing to do with a wedding, that combined with the Woman rune it spoke of a friendship or partnership of some other kind, that the Cup spoke of the tricky choice she had to make, but the Harvest indicated that all would be well. The Sun could mean generosity, but it can also mean a male child...

The obvious answer to the kind neighbour's dilemma sprang straight to our minds at the same moment as we gazed at this spread – why not offer to look after the little boy while his mother worked, as the kind neighbour had young children of her own in any case (this was in the days before CRB checking and other red tape horrors)? Far from being offended, the friend was so very grateful, and years later these two are very close friends who think a lot of one another, and whose children regard one another as family.

Cast Eleven

This cast warned me of a slight road accident I had a few years ago. Next to the Eye lies the Stranger (my own Witchstone), the Crossed Arrows and the Wave, all touching, with the Lightning (my own symbol, speaking of sudden occurrences) lying across them. On my way to the village shop that day I was shunted in the back by a van driver who wasn't paying attention. He was the Stranger, and the accident is shown by the Lightning and Arrows. The Wave meant the loss of my new little car, which I had only bought three weeks earlier, but at least I wasn't hurt.

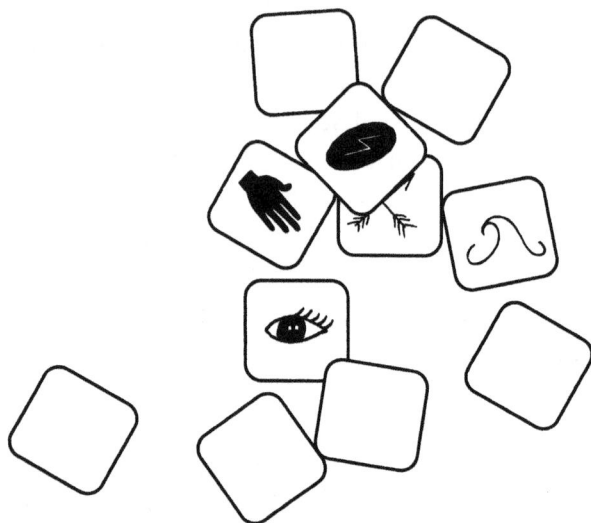

The following simpler readings were done from drawn witchstones; that is the querent put his or her hand into the bag and drew out one Witchstone at a time, rather than casting all the runes onto a cloth.

Cast Twelve

On this morning I drew three Witchstones from the bag and laid them out to see what the day would hold. I had recently moved house, and was now hoping to make new pagan friends in my new area, so was going to the local moot that evening. I was a little anxious; experience had taught me that people at moots could be a mixed bunch, and I was afraid I wouldn't find that I had anything in common with any of them. I got the Rings, the Wave and the Harvest. Thinking that perhaps the reading might refer to something good the next day, and not to the moot, I went along, and was pleased to meet a group of friendly, intelligent people who immediately made me welcome and gave me email addresses and event dates, promised further contacts in the area and invited me to speak at a future moot. Can you understand the significance of these symbols, now that you have started to learn about them? The Rings in this case clearly meant an alliance, rather than romance, that I would form friendships at the moot (actually I ended up going to a larger pagan event with one lady and her husband). The Wave spoke of moving in the right direction on my path, and the Harvest was my reward for making the leap of faith and going along.

Cast Thirteen

Three Witchstones were drawn out and laid in a row, exactly like Tarot cards. The first (reading left to right) represents the querent's past, the second his or her present situation, and the third the outcome that can be expected. In this case the querent drew the Arrows, the Moon and the Sun. Her question had been about her spiritual life – was she doing the right thing by joining a Christian study group in her village? The past, shown by the left hand Witchstone, was the Arrows, which showed how she had sought a path without success, and the Moon showed the choice she had made to find a spiritual path. The Sun indicated that she had made the right choice. This person is now a committed churchgoer and has also built a happy social life through her church contacts.

Cast Fourteen

This drawing was for my husband, who had been offered an interview for a job he really wanted. This opening was indicated by the Cup, my own symbol, which speaks of choices and opportunities. This seems very positive, until you remember that this stone indicates the immediate past that has led to the situation – only positive Witchstones in the present and future positions would mean success, and here the middle and right-hand Witchstones show that disappointment is in store. The Stranger, my own symbol, speaks of the younger man who won the job, and the Wall, my own symbol, speaks of disappointment and obstruction.

I hope these readings have given you some idea of how divination is done using the Witchstones, and demonstrated how the symbols and their relative positions and distances apart influence one another. Learning the symbols and how to interpret them will come easier with time, and I can only emphasize that practice makes perfect – even just a daily reading every morning for yourself will pay dividends in building your skills with the Witchstones.

8. Personalising your Witchstones

Now you have read all about the traditional Witchstones and hopefully have a fair amount of insight into each one, their meanings and messages. Maybe you are already starting to feel that some of them don't really resonate with you, that you can think of symbols that would mean more to you personally. Good! This is a sign that you are starting to develop a good instinct about what you can personally work with, and are starting to get in touch with your inner vision and its language. The important thing about using the Witchstones is your own involvement with them; their messages will come across so much more clearly if you have a relationship with them, know them well.

However, when you are starting out, you need a starting point. My own set began life with 11 Witchstones, Sun, Moon, Rings, Crossed Arrows, Wave, Birds, Harvest, Lightning, Earth, Black Rune and Eye. As you can see, it corresponds fairly roughly to the

91

traditional set of 13, with a few symbols changed here and there. I based it on the symbols given by Marian Green in *The Gentle Arts of Aquarian Magic*, leaving out the symbols I did not really feel were significant or useful, Time and the Whirling Wheel.

Sun, Moon, Rings, Arrows, Wave, Birds, Harvest and Eye are all exactly as in the traditional system of 13. The Lightning corresponds to the Flight/Scythe Witchstone, and carries exactly the same meanings. My set has expanded over the years to 16. This leaves some Witchstones that you have not seen before. I don't plan to discuss these Witchstones from my own set in any great depth, because they are my own symbols, and you may very well decide, when you come to expand your own system, that these mean nothing to you.

Earth

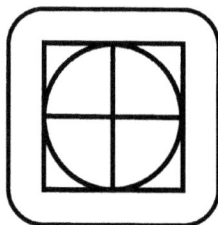

This symbol represents hearth and home. It speaks of safety and security, of the family circle, comfort, protection and the front door slammed and locked against all harm. It is your own armchair in your favourite place by the fire, the teapot on the trivet, your comfort zone. It could even expand to mean near neighbours, but is basically all about the known and safe. It could indicate the physical structure of your home, perhaps even your street or your home town, or somewhere you think of as home even if it isn't any longer where you live, such as your parents' house.

Black Rune/Blank

This Witchstone is simply painted black with no additional symbol on the face (it could equally well have been left completely blank, as I had painted my personal rune signature on the reverse). It essentially means, you won't be told. The Gods won't give you an answer at this time. The workings of karma and the unseen are involved. When I draw this Witchstone, I wait until another day to do another draw or full reading, and see what the day brings.

The Stranger

I made my set of Witchstones from wood, designed them with my own artwork, using colours which I felt were appropriate. I am no Picasso and sometimes it took me two or three tries to get the symbols looking as I wanted them to look. Never mind; I worked at them until they looked all right to me, then varnished them and started to use them.

I started by consecrating my Witchstones in a circle, then went through the process described earlier, of getting to know them one at a time over a period of time. At the full moon I left them on a windowsill overnight to be 'washed' by the moonlight and its energies (this probably sounds a bit off the wall to a non-Wiccan!). The symbols spoke to me and felt right. I carried them with me often, in their drawstring bag; at night I kept them near me (and still do) in my bedside drawer, handy for a quick reading first thing in the morning or, if I was troubled about anything, even in the night.

However, as time went on, and as I did regular readings for myself and for friends, I began to feel there were gaps in the system; things that could not be symbolised by the 11 runes I was using, and that a burden was placed on the existing runes because in many cases they were expected to represent too many factors. Readings were confusing and difficult, meanings overlapped and messages were either too ambiguous or were not easy to understand. The Witchstones seemed to be telling me that they were not complete, that work was still needed on their development. Occasionally, perhaps while driving or working in the garden, an image would come to me of a Witchstone I felt needed adding to my set. Sometimes when I did a reading these extra Witchstones seemed *conspicuous by their absence*, as the saying goes.

After a long time I overcame my scruples about making changes to an ancient system and dared to create...

The first new Witchstone I added was The Stranger. I did not have Man or Woman in my set, and at this stage in my life I knew very little about the witch's runes, had never seen an actual set apart from my own, and did not know of these symbols. It seemed wrong to me that the Sun or the Moon should have to represent human beings on top of all the other information they potentially carry.

So I created the Stranger.

Because the stranger is an unknown quantity I did not want to design it as either a man or a woman. After much thought I created a hooded and robed figure, painted in darkest purple. The moment this was painted I knew it was wrong. The figure looked sinister and threatening instead of just mysterious.

The Stranger represents a meeting with someone new, a new friend just as possibly as a new enemy. It speaks of appearances or intervention by another person, perhaps unknown to you. It certainly is not a bad symbol; like all neutral Witchstones it takes its colour from the runes nearby. It can even mean a new baby.

So I sanded off the portentous hooded figure (he did look a bit like Darth Vader) and replaced him with a simply-drawn human hand. This is quite sexless and could represent any human being, and the symbol is nice because it speaks of a stranger 'taking a hand' in your affairs. In my set it replaces the Man and Woman runestones used in the traditional set of 13. It would also have been quite in order to replace the hooded figure with a simple stick figure or a 'gingerbread man'-type outline, but I liked the idea of the hand. And yes, I agree it isn't the easiest object to draw freehand, but a very simple blob-and-five-sticks drawing will do as long as you know what it is.

After a while the Stranger was joined by others, including the Wheel.

The Wheel

This symbol from Marian Green's set wanted to come back, and I drew it in orange, the colour for travel (that's from our tables of correspondences, and relates to Mercury). Being a Wiccan, I felt the Wheel should also call to mind the Wheel of the Year (the eight festivals that Wiccans celebrate at roughly six-week intervals throughout the seasons), so I drew the Wheel with eight straight spokes. It carries the energies of Mercury, and speaks to me of progress and advancement, of things beginning to move after a period of blockage. It can also have other meanings, such as science, or the past catching you up.

A few years ago I was having a difficult time with a lady in my village Women's Institute, who seemed to resent me, and I was rather upset after receiving news that seemed to imply she had been spreading malicious gossip about me. She had been president, was quite a lot older than me and with old-fashioned attitudes to many things, and seemed to resent younger people who became active in the institute. I turned to my Witchstones for help and inspiration, and drew the Wheel. This was puzzling, as I felt it could hardly give me a 'yes' or 'no' answer to the question in my mind. The next day I drew it again. The next day I concentrated very hard on this lady, and asked if she had been trying to cause trouble for me. Again I drew the Wheel. Shortly afterwards I learned that she had not been the author of the gossip, that she had in fact told the person responsible not to talk nonsense (you know how it is in a village – all sorts of stories get started!). I came to realise that the Wheel's special message is 'move on, think differently'. I learned to think differently about Winifred, and now think of her as a friend, valuing her for some of the very qualities I had formerly disliked. I also learned the valuable lesson that the Witchstones will tell you their meanings if you give them a chance.

The Wall

The next symbol that caught my attention and demanded to be created was the Wall. This symbol I painted in brown, but it has no relation to the Earth symbol and its bricks are strictly symbolic. It carries the energies of Saturn, and speaks to me of obstruction, yet not in the same way as the Arrows. It indicates a blockage of all kinds, including a mental blockage, and is the antithesis of the Wheel. It speaks of limitations, restrictions, hampering, wasted time, obstruction by other people, depression, loss of confidence, barriers, imprisonment, being thwarted by the establishment or others in authority, or even misunderstandings. I often draw this Witchstone when I have to deal with officialdom; anyone who has had to telephone the Driver and Vehicle Licensing Agency and listen to their 25 tiers of recorded options will understand! Recently my husband and I fulfilled one of our dreams and bought a house in Cornwall, but the Gods didn't give us an easy ride. The whole financial situation was a nightmare. Although we had planned and organised all our finances carefully, everything seemed to go wrong at every turn and we were many months delayed in moving in. Time after time I, and my husband, drew this Witchstone, and often the very same day we would hear of another problem that had not been sorted out. 'Delay' is the meaning of this rune, but although it is mildly negative, it also carries the hopeful meaning that walls can be surmounted, and its special message is 'patience'.

The Cup

The Cup was the next symbol I added to my set, because I kept coming up against this symbol wherever I went, and felt it held meaning for me. The cup or chalice is an ancient symbol for choice (as well as being one of the ritual altar tools of Wicca), and this is what this symbol means to me. I painted my Cup in gold, and feel it has the energies of water, the Sun and Venus. It speaks of a choice, a path to a goal ahead. It is a mildly positive rune and also speaks of celebrations – 'my cup runneth over', festivals and sacraments, committal to a path, opportunity, initiation. Its message is 'think carefully before you decide'.

The Apple

The Apple was the last symbol I created, because I did not have the Star of the traditional Witchstones, and I felt its want. I painted it in natural apple colours, green with a red blush on one side, and I feel it carries the energies of the Sun as well as Uranus. The Apple, which has always seemed to me a significant symbol, is a fruit sacred to the Goddess (cut it in half across the middle and you will see Her symbol, the pentagram, in the centre), and in myth and folklore often symbolises a prize or knowledge to be gained. For me it carries all the meaning of the Star rune, as well as speaking of fulfilment, reward, artistic achievement and inspiration. It speaks of health and healing, success and a prize, a gift or nice surprise.

Well that is my own personal experiences on the subject of expanding your system, and now I hope you will feel inspired to think about designing your own Witchstones. It may be you do not resonate with any of the traditional symbols *or* the symbols I have used, in which case it is fine to decide on your own. The possibilities are only limited by your imagination.

If you are an animal lover, why not have a set that uses animals for the symbols? A horse would be a very fine symbol to replace the Wheel, a whale or fish for the Wave, a hare for the Moon and a lion or eagle for the Sun. These images could also be found very easily, if you wanted to use someone else's artwork (or even photographs) to put on your Witchstones.

Or you could use astrological symbols, as long as you stick to a set of 13, including the Eye. See Chapter Two for a list of which Witchstones carry which zodiac signs' energies, though you may have to 'tweak' this a bit.

If you are crazy about flowers, use flowers or plants for the symbols – a rose is the obvious one for the Rings, for example, a sunflower for the Sun, a cactus for the Arrows, seaweed for the Wave, and so on. Use Hollywood stars, chess pieces, cartoon characters or an eclectic collection of symbols drawn from modern culture, or whatever speaks to you and feels right. How about the pantheon of Ancient Egyptian gods, or gods from any other system you feel drawn to?

Think of the board game Monopoly, much loved by families everywhere, and which has gone all over the world and seen its streets changed from the London originals to Dublin, the US's Atlantic City, Milan, Athens or Tokyo. Changing the place names hasn't changed the game or its popularity.

Or you may want to use my own set as a starting point, but feel the meanings are right but not like the designs I have used. Perhaps the Wheel doesn't mean much to you, but you would like a symbol that speaks of travel and movement. So paint a car – or a Harley-Davidson! If you don't like the Arrows, paint a Space Invader, or whatever works for you. No one is looking over your shoulder wagging a finger. Your own personal iconography is the only thing you need to consult to make your choices, and I would be willing to bet that you already have some ideas as to the images you would like to use.

If you don't – and I know it is very frustrating when you want to get started but don't know where to begin, I can only counsel patience. Carry the idea around in your head for a while, and if you still have no inspiration, try forgetting all about the subject for a few days. You may well find that ideas will then come to you. The Goddess doesn't like people tugging at Her hemline saying 'help me' with every little problem (especially when they haven't done much to help themselves), and patience is one of Her virtues. If you try to make it one of yours, She will be more sympathetic to your needs and send you inspiration.

You will probably find that the images come to you one at a time, perhaps at long intervals. When they do, you will recognise them and feel their power, which will prove to you the importance of patience in letting them come to you rather than arbitrarily selecting images.

Whatever you choose to do, make sure you have given it plenty of thought, and have meditated on and got to know your symbols thoroughly, as described earlier.

Happy painting!

9. Witchstones in your Magical Life

This chapter would probably be of most interest to the more experienced Wiccans.

Now that you have spent quite a bit of time on, and with, your Witchstones, making them, carrying them, using them and charging them with your energies, you will find that they take on an energy, a certain magic of their own. They become talismans in their own right. You will find that you want to handle them all the time, that you think about them, and get a 'buzz' from them (if you don't, something is wrong). If you are a Wiccan, you will recognise these feelings from your experience with your witch's equipment, especially your athame. It is part of what makes them effective magical tools. My advice would be that you concentrate on developing this feeling with the Witchstones until you are happy you have developed the best relationship with them that you can. If this means having to re-paint some of the symbols until you are totally pleased with them, so be it.

I have mentioned that it is a very good idea to carry your Witchstones around with you in your daily life, to help them absorb your personal energies. A good way to do this is as part of a "medicine bag", such as Native American shamans might carry, along with other articles that you want to be part of your magical path, such as a dowsing pendulum, dried herbs or crystals that mean something to you, a charm of your animal guide, and so on. Keep the bag fairly small, so you can tuck it into your handbag, pocket or briefcase. If you don't feel happy carrying the bag around with you, perhaps fearing it might fall out of your handbag and reveal its contents to your work colleagues, then hang it beside your bed or your favourite armchair; anywhere you commonly spend time when you are at home.

All this may seem a little like 'playing with toys' to an inexperienced practitioner, but it really makes such a difference to your attitude to and competence with the Witchstones (and what's wrong with playing with toys, anyway?).

A Wiccan or other pagan working magic would have on the altar herbs, crystals, coloured candles, incense and other 'props' chosen for their relevance to the work in hand. Under the system of magical correspondences, colours, perfumes, plants and other substances are listed as appropriate to attract certain energies, or items can be used as the focus of the spell or charged by chanting and concentration. A High Priestess or High Priest can supercharge an item with the energies of the circle as she or he breaks it down at the end of the ritual; to a lesser extent this can be done by a solitary practitioner. Such an item can then be carried on the person as a talisman to continue the magical working to its conclusion. The Witchstones can certainly be used just like an individual crystal or other talisman as the focus of a spell. Try the Sun for success in a job interview, the Rings to bring a new friendship, the Romance to bring love into your life or the Ear of Corn for general success and achievement. Waiting to hear from a friend? Carry the Birds, charged with the energies of Mercury.

Because you also need to keep your Witchstones together in their bag for readings, you can make a facsimile of the Witchstone you need to use, from sturdy cardboard or a small piece of wood. It doesn't need to be as polished as the Witchstones you have made for readings, but it should still be consecrated. These facsimiles have the advantage that they can be pierced and threaded on a chain, ribbon or thong and worn on the person, but the disadvantage that they lack the personal empowerment capabilities of your own Witchstones. If you felt that you would be using the Witchstones very often in magical work, it might be worth your while to actually make two sets, one for divination and one for spellworking, giving them both the full consecration and personalisation described in earlier chapters, but perhaps making one set with piercings so they can be worn.

The Futhark runes can be used to write spells because they are alphabetical, and because there is a sound associated with each one, they can be used for chanting and other magical calls. The Witchstones do not have these lingual properties, but there is nothing to stop you from developing chants based on the symbols. If, for example, you were using the Wave stone as a focus for a spell about travel, you might make up a verse that was easy to recite and contained key words associated with the Wave symbol.

'Wave of glory, blue and bright, work my will this moonlit night' isn't Wordsworth, but it is easy to chant and helps focus your mind on the working to build power.

When casting a circle the Witchstones may even be useful if you are short on tools – perhaps when doing a working away from home when you have not brought your "kit". The Moon and Sun may be used on the altar to represent the Goddess and God, while the Ear of Corn, the Birds, the Arrows and the Wave may be used to mark the four cardinal points, or used as the substances for these elements and carried around during reinforcement of the circle.

Spells can be found in just about any magic book you find and on a thousand websites, so I won't give too much space to them, but here are two simple spells to illustrate the way in which you might use the Witchstones. When casting a spell, make sure you have all the items you need to hand, that you have your goal firmly fixed in your mind and that you have any chant or rhyme needed for the spell written down (or memorised). But by far the important thing to remember for spell-casting is that your own attitude is what matters the most. If you go into a circle and cast a spell while full of positive energy and confidence in your own powers you will be far more likely to succeed than if you do it half-heartedly, with the attitude that "it probably won't work, but I'll try it anyway". In just the same way that thoughts and mental attitudes colour and influence your everyday life, they will also affect any magical work you may undertake. Think of your Witchstones, the buzz they give you, and take that empowerment with you into any magical workings you may do. That is a tool as potent as the shiniest athame you can own.

A Simple Spell to Attract Romance into Your Life

You will need:

A pink or green candle.

Rose or patchouli incense (or if you don't have these, anything sweet).

Pink rose petals – these can be dried if you don't have fresh.

The Romance Witchstone, or a facsimile made from cardboard or wood.

On a Friday light the pink candle and light the incense. Make a pile of the rose petals on a plate or basket. Take time to ground and centre yourself, holding the Romance in your hands. There is no need to concentrate on it, but be aware that you are holding it and that it is a talisman to help you achieve your aims. When you are perfectly centred raise the Romance to your chest and press it against your heart, repeating the following chant:

"By the rose's petals fine,
Love is coming, love is mine."

When you feel that the power has been raised (recognising this takes some practice, but you will get better at it), say:

"I am now fully open to romance entering my life. I will
soon find love. So mote it be."

Spend some time imagining yourself meeting the right person – really see this as happening and know it is true. Lay the Romance in the rose petals, blow out the candle, then get up and leave the room, go and have something to eat and drink and think about something else. When you return to the room, pick up the Romance and carry it with you as a charm to attract love. Offer the rose petals to the Goddess if you wish, or recycle them in the compost. Feel confident and sure that love is coming to you.

This spell can be repeated as often as you wish.

A Simple Spell for Success in a Job Interview

You will need:

A bright yellow or gold candle.

An item to represent the job you are going after, such as a picture of the office building, a notepad or a sheet of copier paper for an office job, or even a small stone taken from the work site.

A good pinch of ground cinnamon.

The Sun Witchstone or its facsimile.

Light the gold candle on a Sunday and place it on and close to the item representing the job you are trying to get. Take the Sun Witchstone in your hand and think your wishes into it very hard for a moment or two, then add it on top of the item. Cast the cinnamon over this little pile, saying:

> *"Spice and candle, mighty Sun,*
> *By your powers my job is won."*

Spend some time sitting in front of the gold candle, visualising yourself in the job and having plenty of money, and knowing this will be true. Then get up and leave the room, have something to eat and think about something else. The candle should be left to burn down, so you may want to transfer it to a wide tray or large bowl for safety. Carry the Sun with you when you go for your interview and for several days afterwards. You might also want to carry it when you arrive for your first day at work, to ensure all goes smoothly.

By now you will be more accustomed to using meditation techniques, such as the breathing relaxation in the chapter on using your runes, but you can also take this a step further and meditate with your Witchstones, or use them as pathworking aids. If you are not accustomed to meditation (or even if you are!) you may find that your conscious mind throws up difficulties with this discipline, interrupting you constantly with "chatter", images, reminders of things you have to do and memories. It is very hard, particularly for a beginner, to gently push away this mental static and return to the altered state. Gurus throughout the ages have come up with techniques for slowing the mind and keeping the conscious, everyday mind occupied with something else so that it does not interfere. Breathing and physical relaxation techniques, fingering rosaries, chanting and staring at objects or pictures are all recommended. Being small, smooth and tactile, your witchstones will be useful in many ways for meditation, including as "worry-stones" to stroke between your fingers to help still your mind, and the symbols can also be kept before the eye to concentrate the mind, perhaps using the appropriate symbol suitable for a meditation on a particular subject. Using them like this will also increase their empowerment abilities for you still more.

The individual witchstones can also be used for pathworkings or guided meditations, literally holding the selected witchstone in your hand and taking it into the realm of your pathworking.

Here is an example taken from my own Book of Shadows (a witch's magical journal), using the Flight Witchstone in an Ostara meditation for new beginnings:

> *The Flight is a neutral Witchstone, and speaks of sudden change. This will be the change you plan to make in yourself – your "New Year's Resolution" for Ostara, which you must*

107

keep in mind as you go on. Perhaps it is a determination to change something you dislike about yourself, such as bad temper or a tendency to judge others, or it may be the desire to change your body by losing weight or changing your lifestyle to become fitter. Or it may even be something more life-changing, such as the knowledge that you must end a destructive relationship – or take a new relationship that is working out well to the next level.

Close your eyes, relax, ground and centre. Have the Flight stone in your hand as a talisman, and be aware of it leading you where you need to go.

You are walking up a gentle slope. The air is blowing lightly around you and the light is pale yellow. Walk on. The grass is soft, so you stop and take off your shoes and socks to walk barefoot; the grass is so inviting and slightly damp under your feet.

Walk on until you reach the brow of the hill; the air is full of delicious floral scents now. As you reach the hilltop, you see that before you lies a broad meadow, yellow with delicate spring flowers, stretching away as far as you can see. Enjoy the beauty of the scene. As you stand there, two figures come into your vision, approaching you from the other end of the field. You feel peaceful and relaxed, as they approach, one some way in front of the other.

The first figure draws up to you now, and you go down to meet her, running down a short slope and into the meadow. She is a beautiful lady wearing a gold and green dress, with long, corn-coloured hair hanging down over her shoulders and back. As you approach her, you see she is very much taller than you, so that you have to look upwards into her face. She is very beautiful, more beautiful than anyone you have ever seen. You can see that her dress is actually made, not from cloth, but from green living things, grasses, leaves and tendrils, interlaced with real live spring flowers.

Greet her and speak to her; she is your Mother. Tell her all that you hope for in the coming summer, of the change you hope to effect within yourself, in the knowledge that she will listen and will help you, if it is in your highest interest. Show her the Flight talisman you carry in your hand. She touches the witchstone with the tip of her finger, then nods knowingly and smiles her understanding. Perhaps she speaks – take note of all she does or says.

When you have spoken to her, she moves on, turning across the field and moving away.

The second person now catches up to you. He is a young man, more beautiful than anyone you ever met, with corn-coloured hair and very blue eyes, dressed in light garments made from grasses and flowers.

Greet him and speak to him; although he is timelessly young, he is your Father. Tell him of your fears and worries for the coming year, as you would tell your own father, in the knowledge that he will listen and help. Tell him how you wish to change yourself. Show him the Flight; he will touch it and nod as before. If he speaks, take note of this as well.

When you have spoken, he turns away and follows the Goddess on her way. Watch them go across the beautiful field, then turn and make your way back up the slope and down the further side to where you have left your shoes and socks.

Return.

This pathworking is only one example. It may not mean anything to you, and or there may elements about it you would like to change so that it suits your own circumstances. Perhaps you are black, for example, and would like your Goddess and God to be black also – then so they should be. Or perhaps you are an urbanite who cannot identify with the rural scene described above, in which case you should design your pathworking to suit what feels right for you.

Of course, you can select any Witchstone to take with you, depending on the purpose of the meditation or pathworking; you may even take several, and use them in different ways as you explore the other realms. A time may come when you do not need to focus on taking them with you because you find they are already with you. Then you will know the Witchstones have truly become a part of you and given you their blessings. Now you can consider yourself a true practitioner of an ancient art.

The Witchstones can also be used with other magical tools, such as a dowsing pendulum. For a quick answer to a question lay out the appropriate Witchstones, a little apart, and ask your question. Then hold your pendulum over the symbols and see what it indicates. Dowsing with a pendulum is very easy and requires very little knowledge. Like the Witchstones (and many other magical tools) your pendulum should be personal to you, but it is easily made from a fragment of stone, a crystal or a piece of wood, hung from a small chain or piece of string. I have a lovely pendulum made from a small holed stone found in the garden and strung on a ribbon, which works just as well as the carved and shaped piece of green aventurine strung on a silver chain that I treated myself to at the crystal shop, and certainly cost a lot less. Generally speaking you should ask your pendulum to show you your "yes" and your "no" before you start, if you are asking a question that will be answered in this way and unless you are very familiar with the art. The pendulum will swing one way for yes and another for no, perhaps one as a straight line and the other as a circling movement, and you are then ready to ask your question. A question that might be answered by choice, rather than by yes or no, is asked by holding the pendulum over the Witchstones and noting which way it swings. To give a very simple example, you might have just moved to a new town and have the choice of two doctors' surgeries to go and register with. You don't know the area and have no idea which to choose. Select a Witchstone to represent them both – perhaps this will be as easy as taking the Man and Woman symbol because the doctors are of different genders – and lay these out for the pendulum to indicate.

There will be many more ways, as you travel your magical path, in which you will find the Witchstones are of use, but perhaps their most important gift to you will be the opening of your eyes to things that are other than this reality in which we walk, breathe and perceive. Whatever paths they lead you on, may the Goddess take you by the hand and guide you, giving you no more vision than you have wisdom to receive, but helping that wisdom to grow always. Blessed be.

www.ingramcontent.com/pod-product-compliance
Lightning Source LLC
Chambersburg PA
CBHW051741090426
42738CB00010B/2368